Nicolas De Crécy

Glacial Period

MUSÉE DU
LOUVRE
ÉDITIONS

ISBN 10: 1-56163-483-2
ISBN 13: 978-1-56163-483-5
© Futuropolis/Musee du Louvre Editions 2005
©2006 NBM for the English translation
Translation by Joe Johnson
Lettering by Ortho
Printed in Hong Kong

5 4 3 2 1

ComicsLit is an imprint
and trademark of

NANTIER · BEALL · MINOUSTCHINE
Publishing inc.
new york

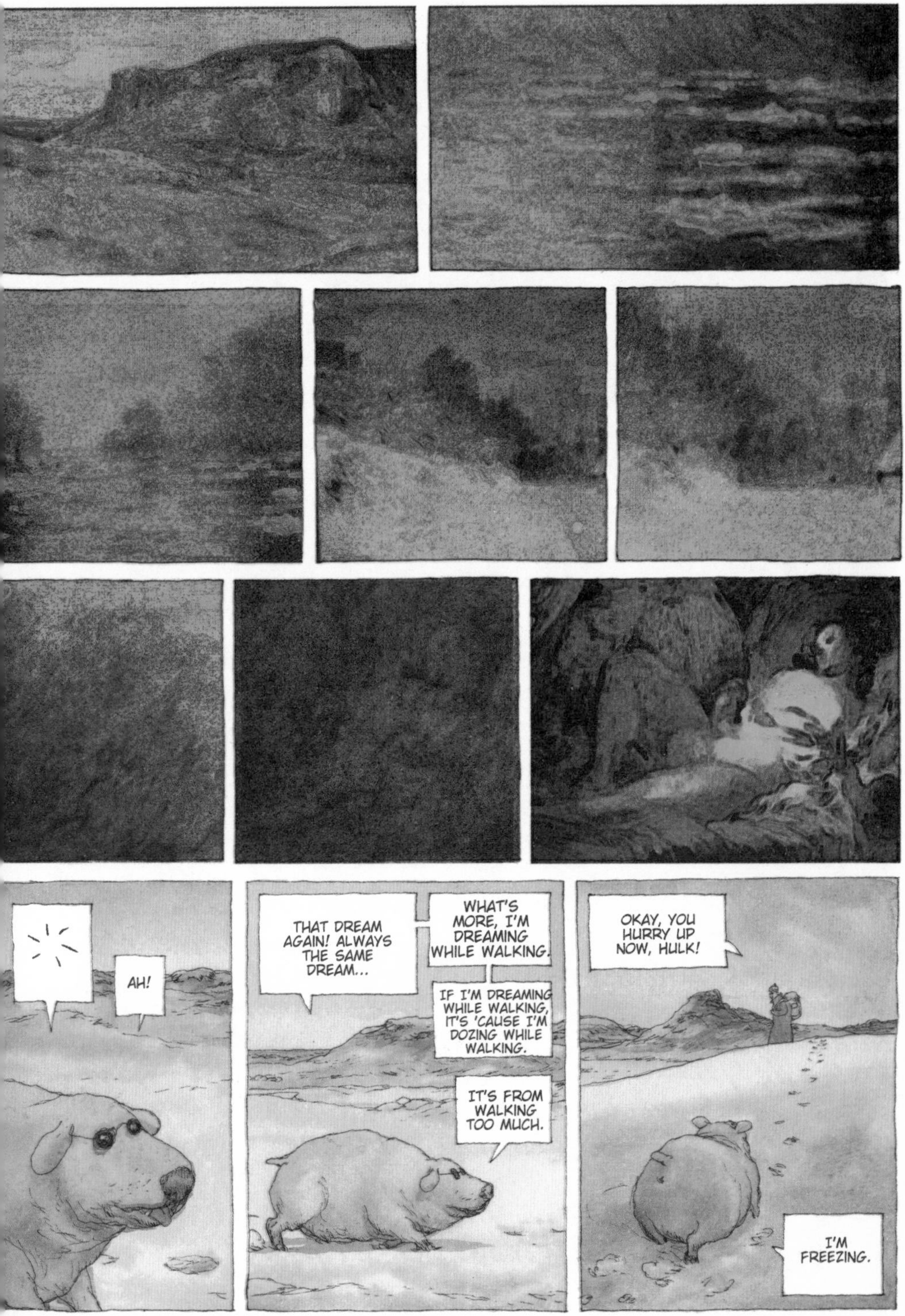
AH!
THAT DREAM AGAIN! ALWAYS THE SAME DREAM...
WHAT'S MORE, I'M DREAMING WHILE WALKING.
IF I'M DREAMING WHILE WALKING, IT'S 'CAUSE I'M DOZING WHILE WALKING.
IT'S FROM WALKING TOO MUCH.
OKAY, YOU HURRY UP NOW, HULK!
I'M FREEZING.

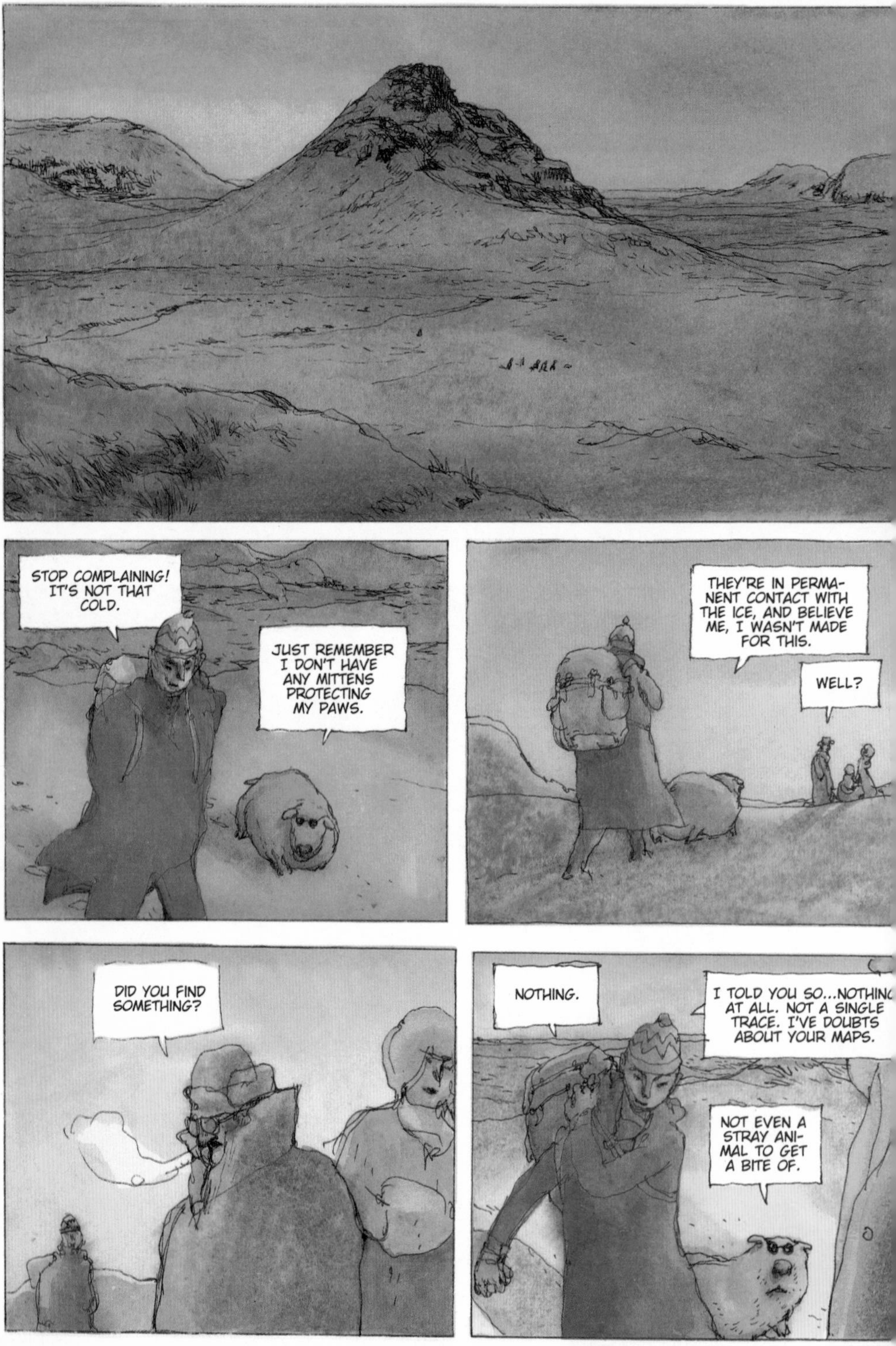
STOP COMPLAINING! IT'S NOT THAT COLD.
JUST REMEMBER I DON'T HAVE ANY MITTENS PROTECTING MY PAWS.
THEY'RE IN PERMA-NENT CONTACT WITH THE ICE, AND BELIEVE ME, I WASN'T MADE FOR THIS.
WELL?
DID YOU FIND SOMETHING?
NOTHING.
I TOLD YOU SO...NOTHING AT ALL. NOT A SINGLE TRACE. I'VE DOUBTS ABOUT YOUR MAPS.
NOT EVEN A STRAY ANI-MAL TO GET A BITE OF.

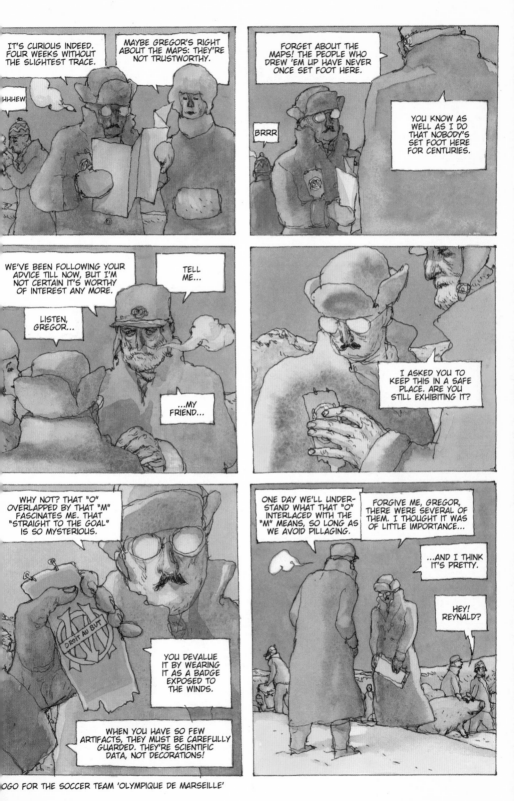

IT'S CURIOUS INDEED. FOUR WEEKS WITHOUT THE SLIGHTEST TRACE.

MAYBE GREGOR'S RIGHT ABOUT THE MAPS: THEY'RE NOT TRUSTWORTHY.

HHHEW

FORGET ABOUT THE MAPS! THE PEOPLE WHO DREW 'EM UP HAVE NEVER ONCE SET FOOT HERE.

BRRR

YOU KNOW AS WELL AS I DO THAT NOBODY'S SET FOOT HERE FOR CENTURIES.

WE'VE BEEN FOLLOWING YOUR ADVICE TILL NOW, BUT I'M NOT CERTAIN IT'S WORTHY OF INTEREST ANY MORE.

TELL ME...

LISTEN, GREGOR...

...MY FRIEND...

I ASKED YOU TO KEEP THIS IN A SAFE PLACE. ARE YOU STILL EXHIBITING IT?

WHY NOT? THAT "O" OVERLAPPED BY THAT "M" FASCINATES ME. THAT "STRAIGHT TO THE GOAL" IS SO MYSTERIOUS.

DROIT AU BUT

YOU DEVALUE IT BY WEARING IT AS A BADGE EXPOSED TO THE WINDS.

WHEN YOU HAVE SO FEW ARTIFACTS, THEY MUST BE CAREFULLY GUARDED. THEY'RE SCIENTIFIC DATA, NOT DECORATIONS!

ONE DAY WE'LL UNDER-STAND WHAT THAT "O" INTERLACED WITH THE "M" MEANS, SO LONG AS WE AVOID PILLAGING.

FORGIVE ME, GREGOR, THERE WERE SEVERAL OF THEM. I THOUGHT IT WAS OF LITTLE IMPORTANCE...

...AND I THINK IT'S PRETTY.

HEY! REYNALD?

OGO FOR THE SOCCER TEAM 'OLYMPIQUE DE MARSEILLE'

5

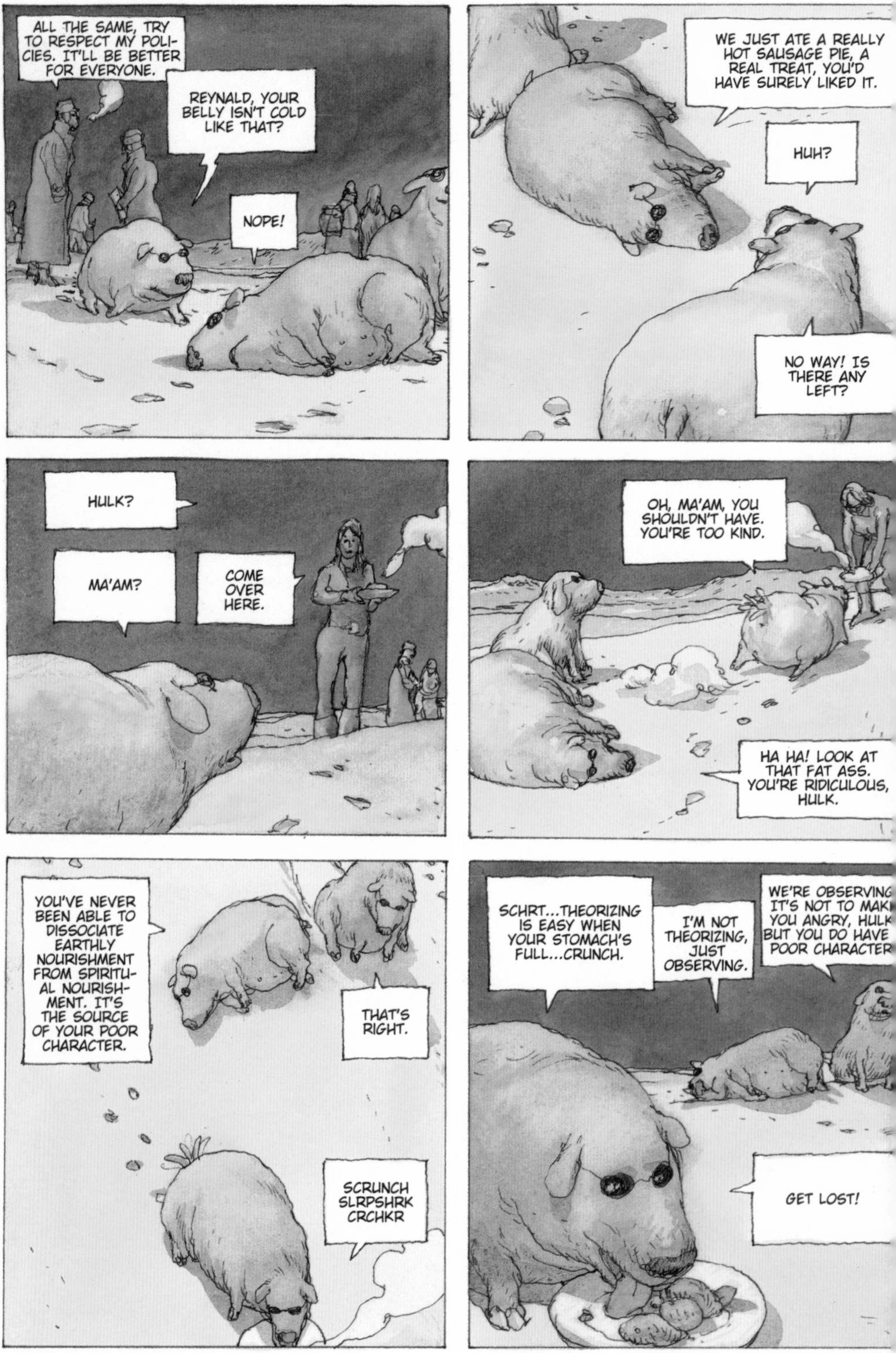
ALL THE SAME, TRY TO RESPECT MY POLICIES. IT'LL BE BETTER FOR EVERYONE.
REYNALD, YOUR BELLY ISN'T COLD LIKE THAT?
NOPE!
WE JUST ATE A REALLY HOT SAUSAGE PIE, A REAL TREAT, YOU'D HAVE SURELY LIKED IT.
HUH?
NO WAY! IS THERE ANY LEFT?
HULK?
MA'AM?
COME OVER HERE.
OH, MA'AM, YOU SHOULDN'T HAVE. YOU'RE TOO KIND.
HA HA! LOOK AT THAT FAT ASS. YOU'RE RIDICULOUS, HULK.
YOU'VE NEVER BEEN ABLE TO DISSOCIATE EARTHLY NOURISHMENT FROM SPIRITUAL NOURISHMENT. IT'S THE SOURCE OF YOUR POOR CHARACTER.
THAT'S RIGHT.
SCRUNCH SLRPSHRK CRCHKR
SCHRT...THEORIZING IS EASY WHEN YOUR STOMACH'S FULL...CRUNCH.
I'M NOT THEORIZING, JUST OBSERVING.
WE'RE OBSERVING IT'S NOT TO MAK YOU ANGRY, HULK BUT YOU DO HAVE POOR CHARACTER
GET LOST!

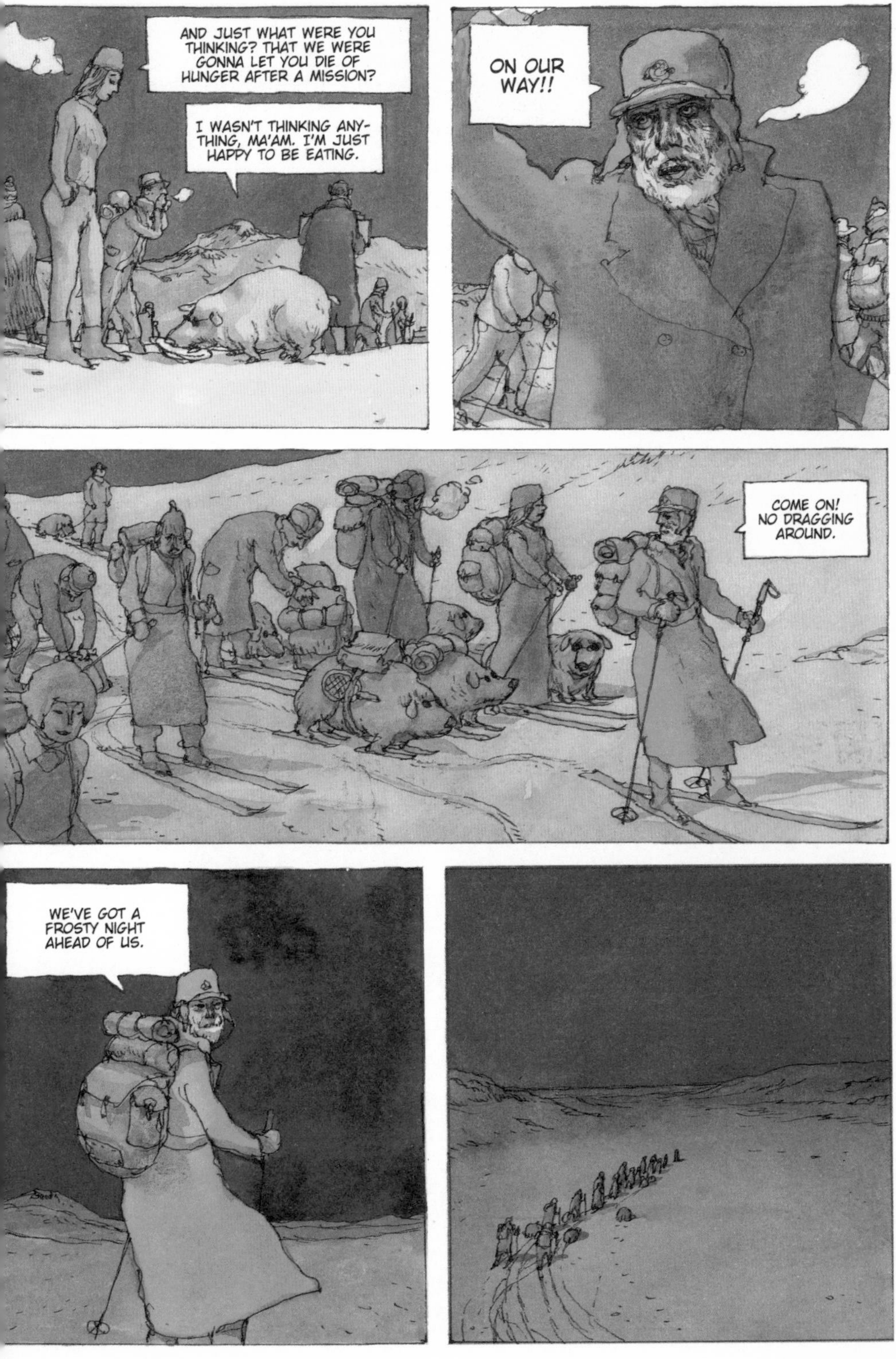
AND JUST WHAT WERE YOU THINKING? THAT WE WERE GONNA LET YOU DIE OF HUNGER AFTER A MISSION?
I WASN'T THINKING ANY-THING, MA'AM. I'M JUST HAPPY TO BE EATING.
ON OUR WAY!!
COME ON! NO DRAGGING AROUND.
WE'VE GOT A FROSTY NIGHT AHEAD OF US.

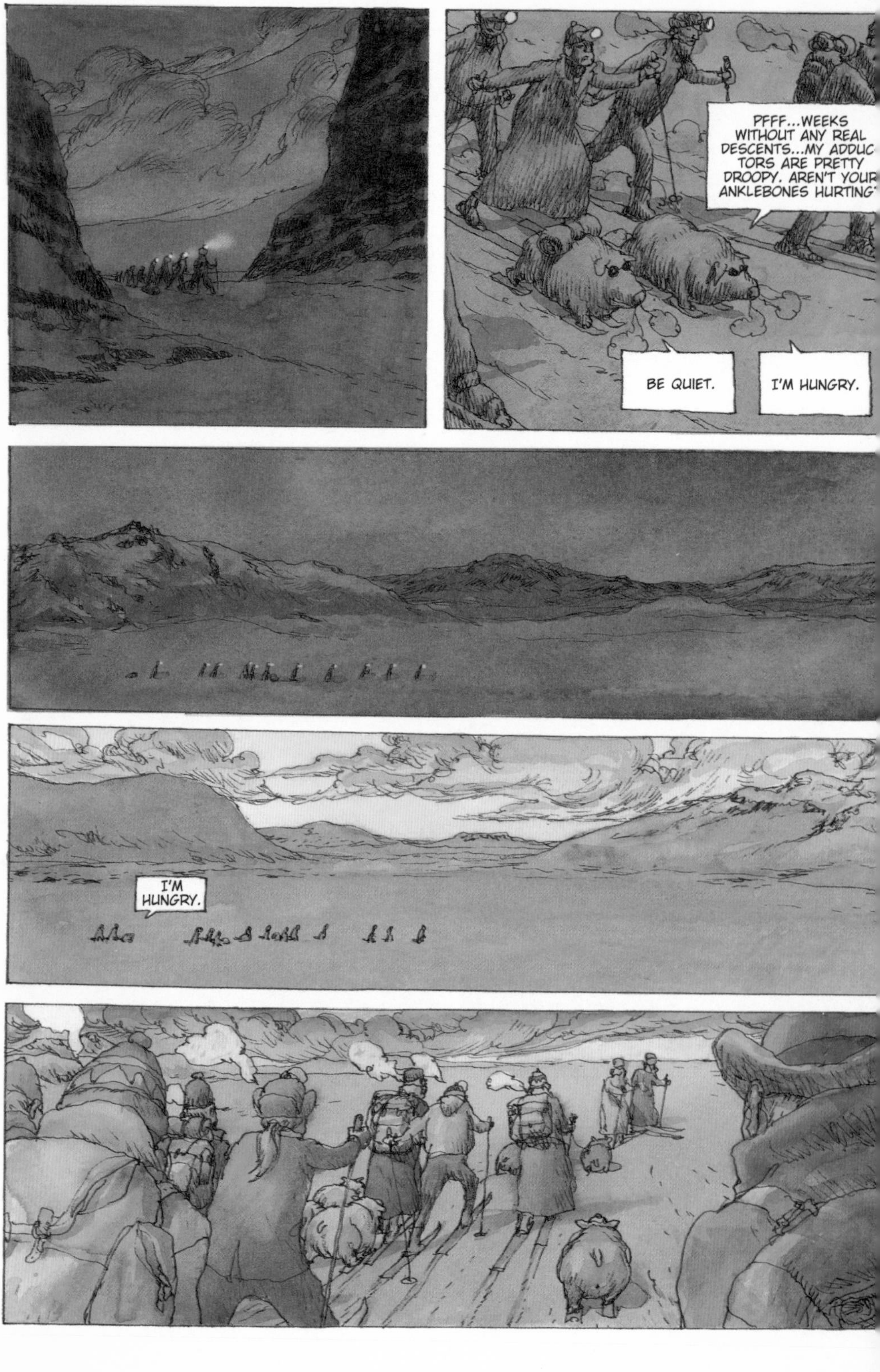
PFFF...WEEKS WITHOUT ANY REAL DESCENTS...MY ADDUC TORS ARE PRETTY DROOPY. AREN'T YOUR ANKLEBONES HURTING
BE QUIET.
I'M HUNGRY.
I'M HUNGRY.

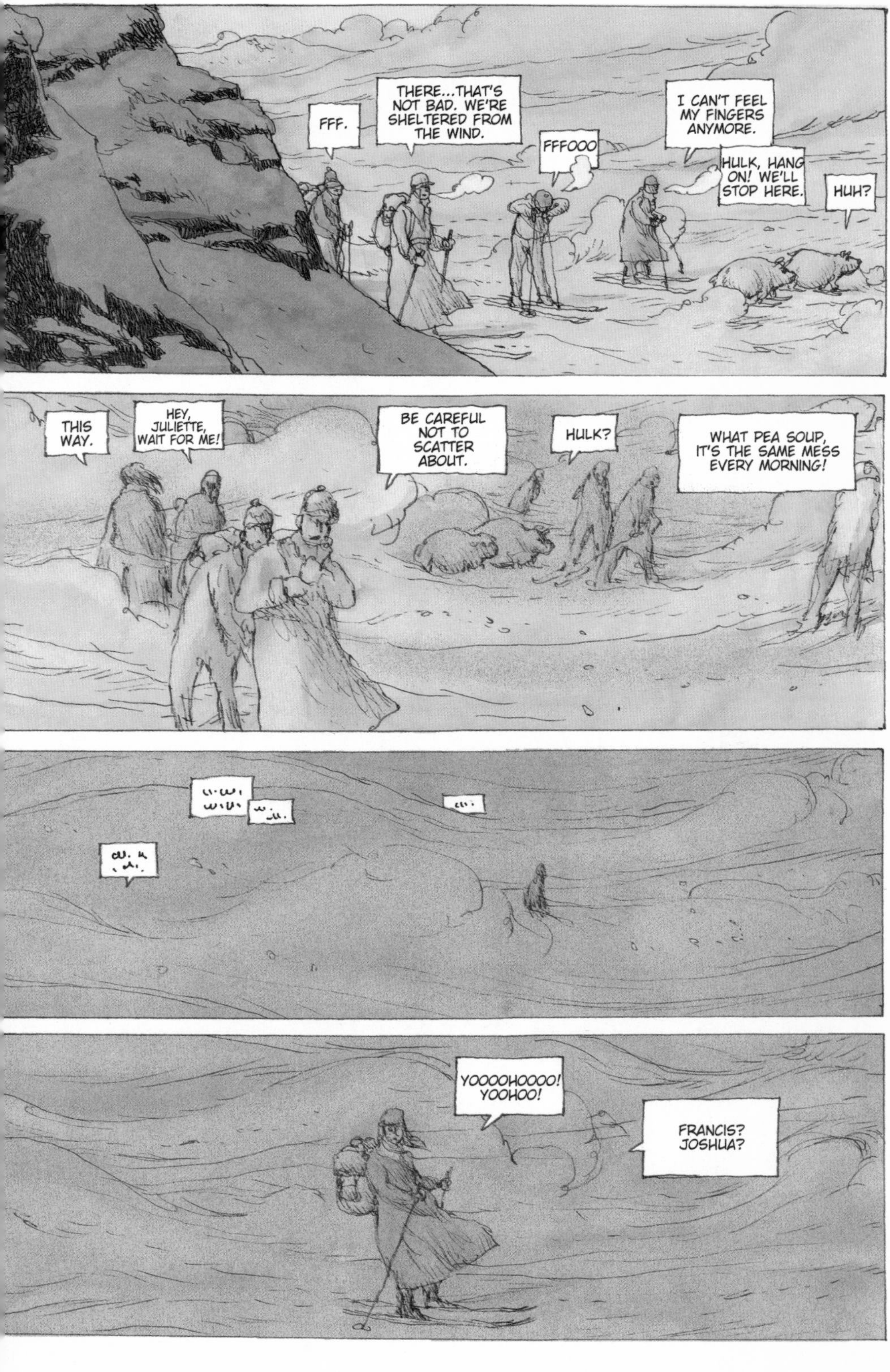
FFF.
THERE...THAT'S NOT BAD. WE'RE SHELTERED FROM THE WIND.
FFFOOO
I CAN'T FEEL MY FINGERS ANYMORE.
HULK, HANG ON! WE'LL STOP HERE.
HUH?
THIS WAY.
HEY, JULIETTE, WAIT FOR ME!
BE CAREFUL NOT TO SCATTER ABOUT.
HULK?
WHAT PEA SOUP, IT'S THE SAME MESS EVERY MORNING!
YOOOOHOOOO! YOOHOO!
FRANCIS? JOSHUA?

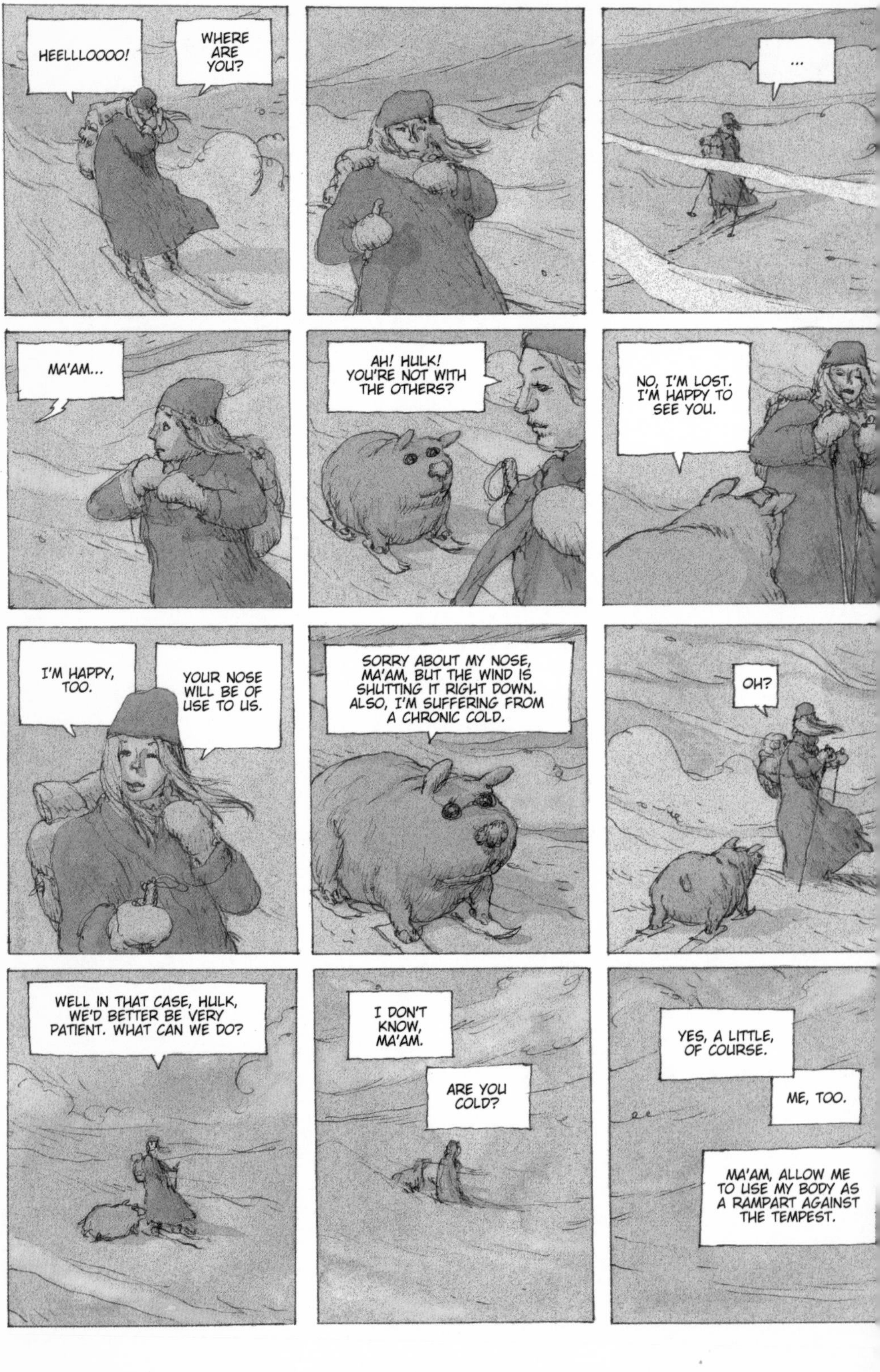
HEELLLOOOO!
WHERE ARE YOU?
...
MA'AM...
AH! HULK! YOU'RE NOT WITH THE OTHERS?
NO, I'M LOST. I'M HAPPY TO SEE YOU.
I'M HAPPY, TOO.
YOUR NOSE WILL BE OF USE TO US.
SORRY ABOUT MY NOSE, MA'AM, BUT THE WIND IS SHUTTING IT RIGHT DOWN. ALSO, I'M SUFFERING FROM A CHRONIC COLD.
OH?
WELL IN THAT CASE, HULK, WE'D BETTER BE VERY PATIENT. WHAT CAN WE DO?
I DON'T KNOW, MA'AM.
ARE YOU COLD?
YES, A LITTLE, OF COURSE.
ME, TOO.
MA'AM, ALLOW ME TO USE MY BODY AS A RAMPART AGAINST THE TEMPEST.

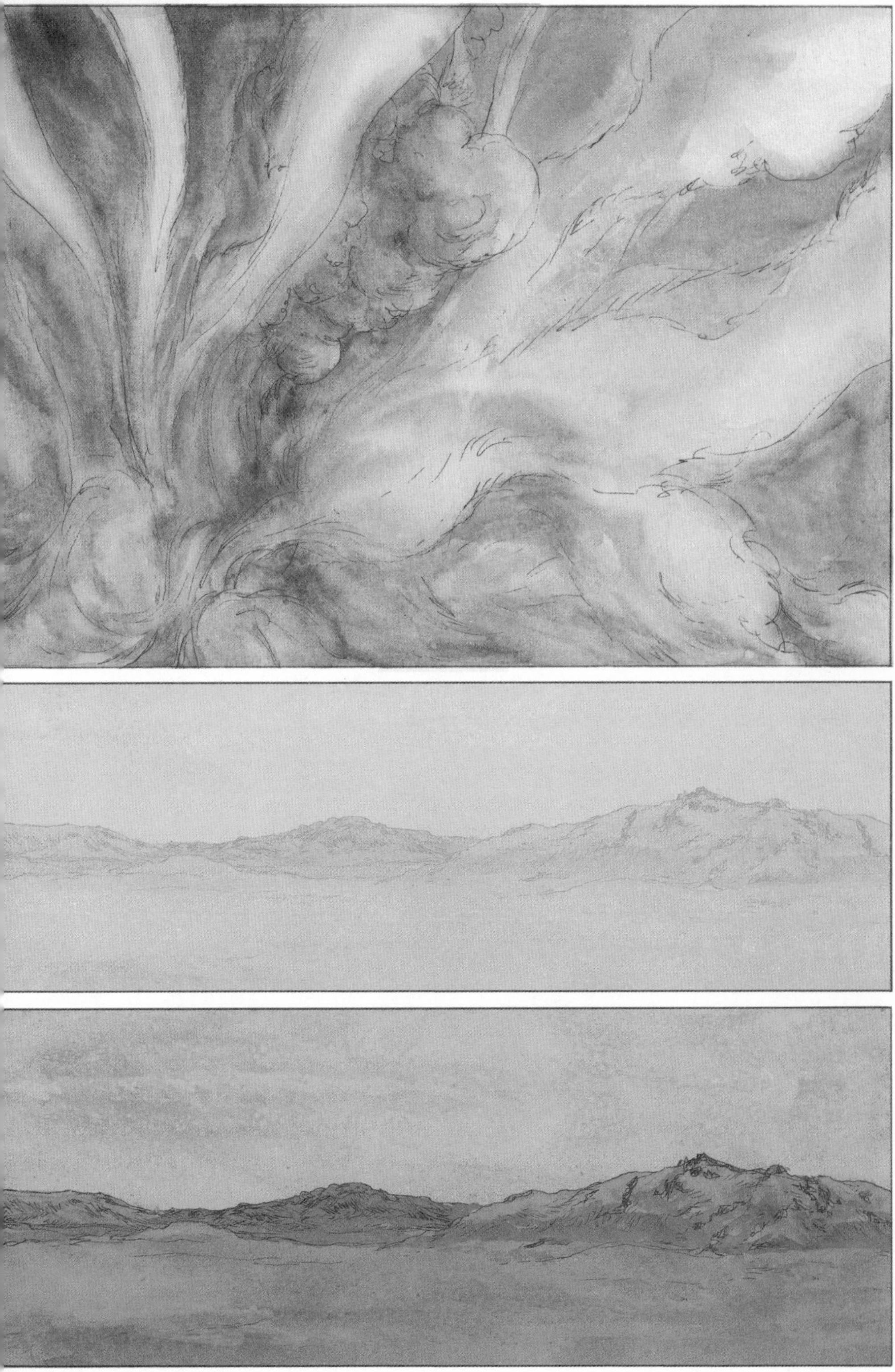

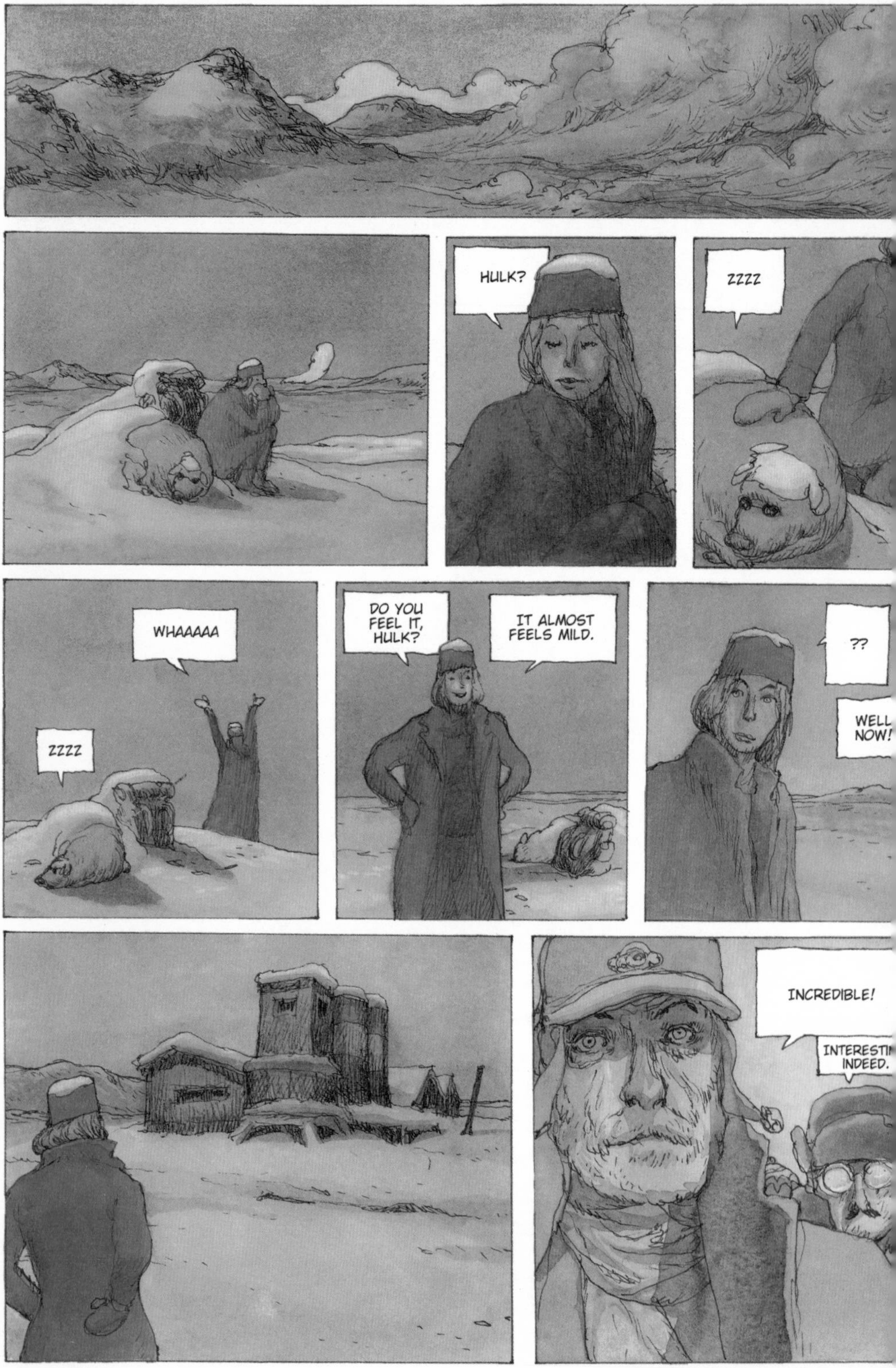
HULK?
ZZZZ
WHAAAAA
ZZZZ
DO YOU FEEL IT, HULK?
IT ALMOST FEELS MILD.
??
WELL NOW!
INCREDIBLE!
INTERESTI INDEED.

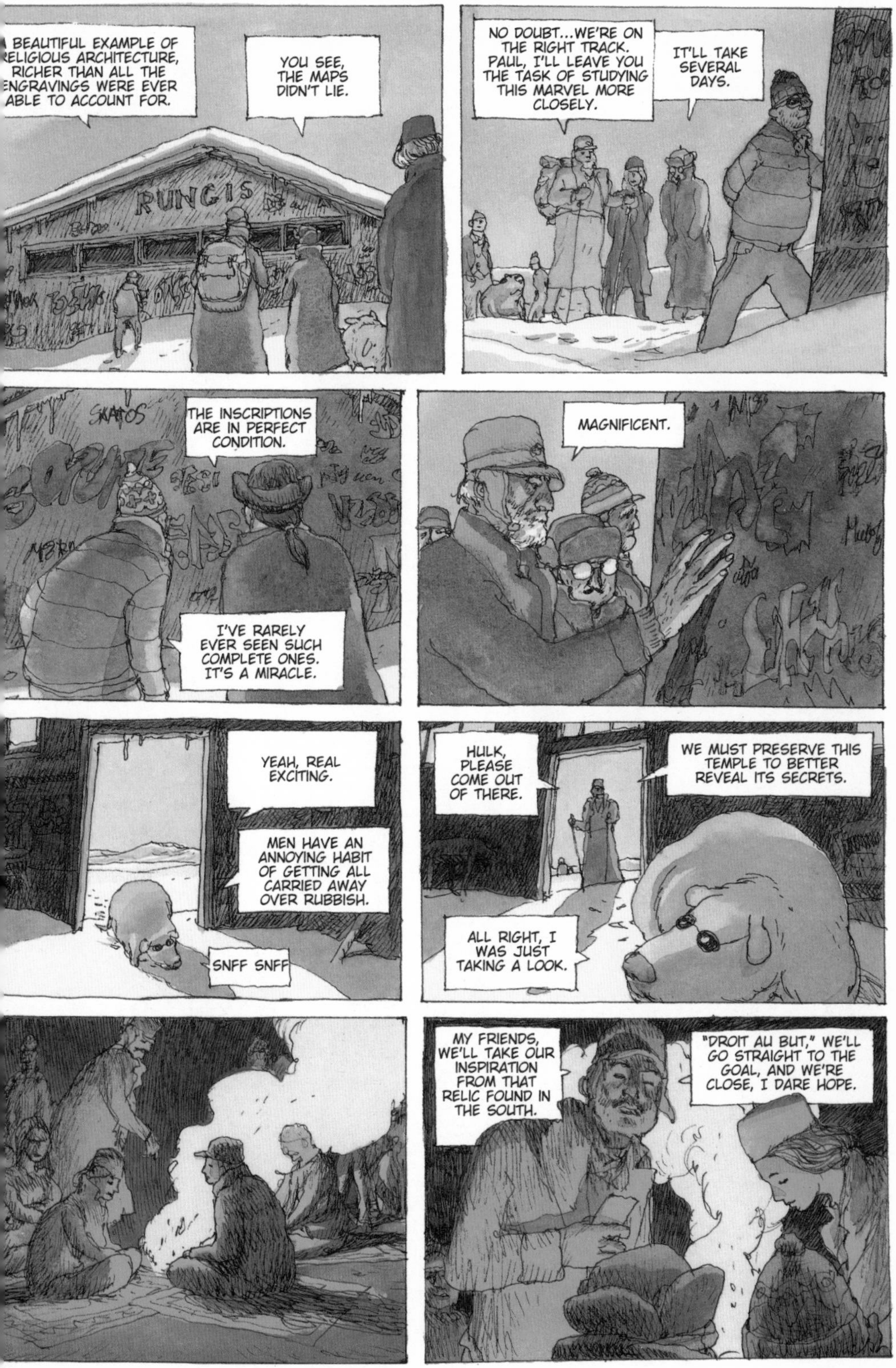
A BEAUTIFUL EXAMPLE OF RELIGIOUS ARCHITECTURE, RICHER THAN ALL THE ENGRAVINGS WERE EVER ABLE TO ACCOUNT FOR.
YOU SEE, THE MAPS DIDN'T LIE.
RUNGIS
NO DOUBT...WE'RE ON THE RIGHT TRACK. PAUL, I'LL LEAVE YOU THE TASK OF STUDYING THIS MARVEL MORE CLOSELY.
IT'LL TAKE SEVERAL DAYS.
THE INSCRIPTIONS ARE IN PERFECT CONDITION.
I'VE RARELY EVER SEEN SUCH COMPLETE ONES. IT'S A MIRACLE.
MAGNIFICENT.
YEAH, REAL EXCITING.
MEN HAVE AN ANNOYING HABIT OF GETTING ALL CARRIED AWAY OVER RUBBISH.
SNFF SNFF
HULK, PLEASE COME OUT OF THERE.
WE MUST PRESERVE THIS TEMPLE TO BETTER REVEAL ITS SECRETS.
ALL RIGHT, I WAS JUST TAKING A LOOK.
MY FRIENDS, WE'LL TAKE OUR INSPIRATION FROM THAT RELIC FOUND IN THE SOUTH.
"DROIT AU BUT," WE'LL GO STRAIGHT TO THE GOAL, AND WE'RE CLOSE, I DARE HOPE.

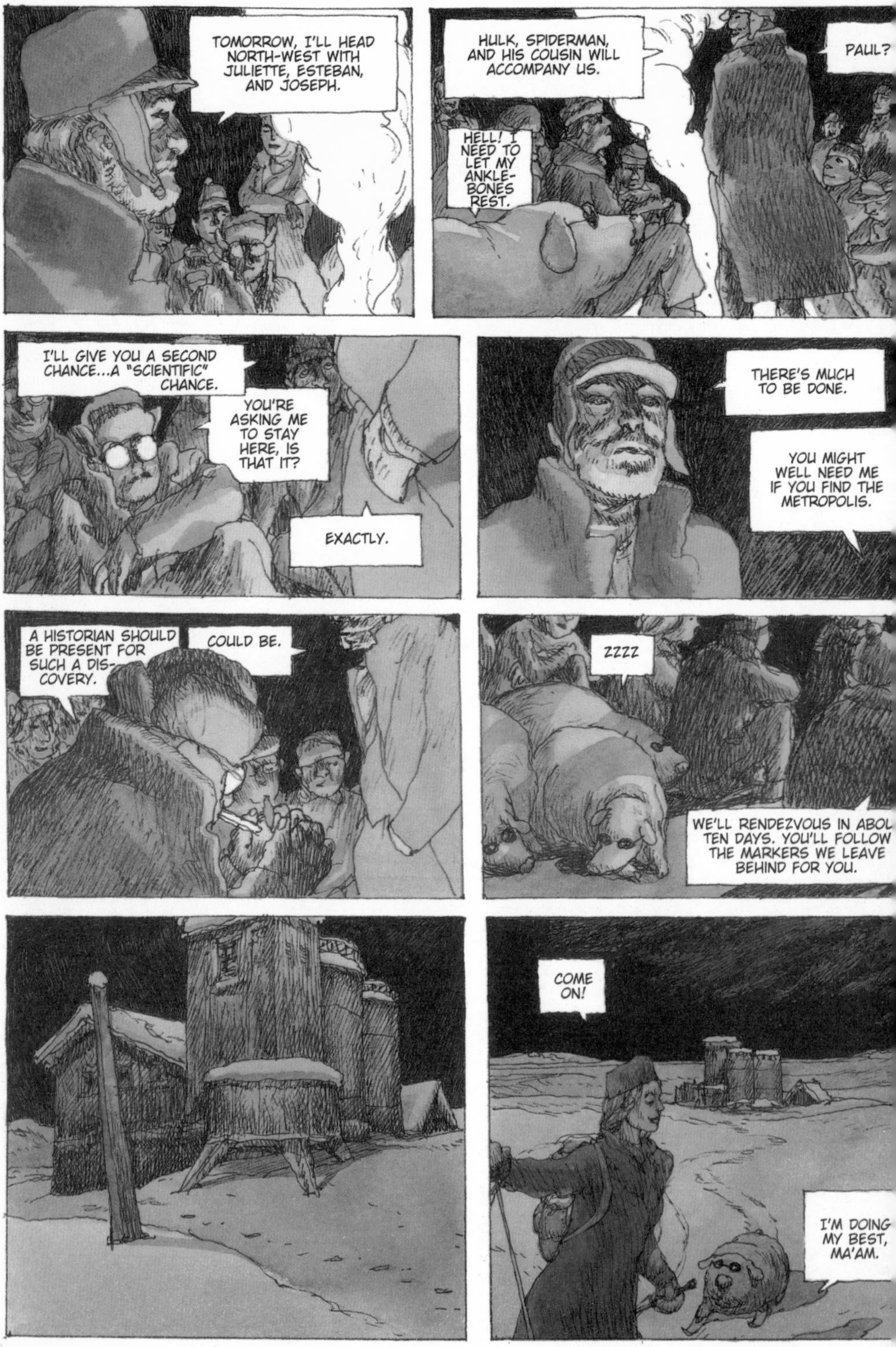
TOMORROW, I'LL HEAD NORTH-WEST WITH JULIETTE, ESTEBAN, AND JOSEPH.
HULK, SPIDERMAN, AND HIS COUSIN WILL ACCOMPANY US.
HELL! I NEED TO LET MY ANKLE-BONES REST.
PAUL?
I'LL GIVE YOU A SECOND CHANCE...A "SCIENTIFIC" CHANCE.
YOU'RE ASKING ME TO STAY HERE, IS THAT IT?
EXACTLY.
THERE'S MUCH TO BE DONE.
YOU MIGHT WELL NEED ME IF YOU FIND THE METROPOLIS.
A HISTORIAN SHOULD BE PRESENT FOR SUCH A DIS-COVERY.
COULD BE.
ZZZZ
WE'LL RENDEZVOUS IN ABOU TEN DAYS. YOU'LL FOLLOW THE MARKERS WE LEAVE BEHIND FOR YOU.
COME ON!
I'M DOING MY BEST, MA'AM.

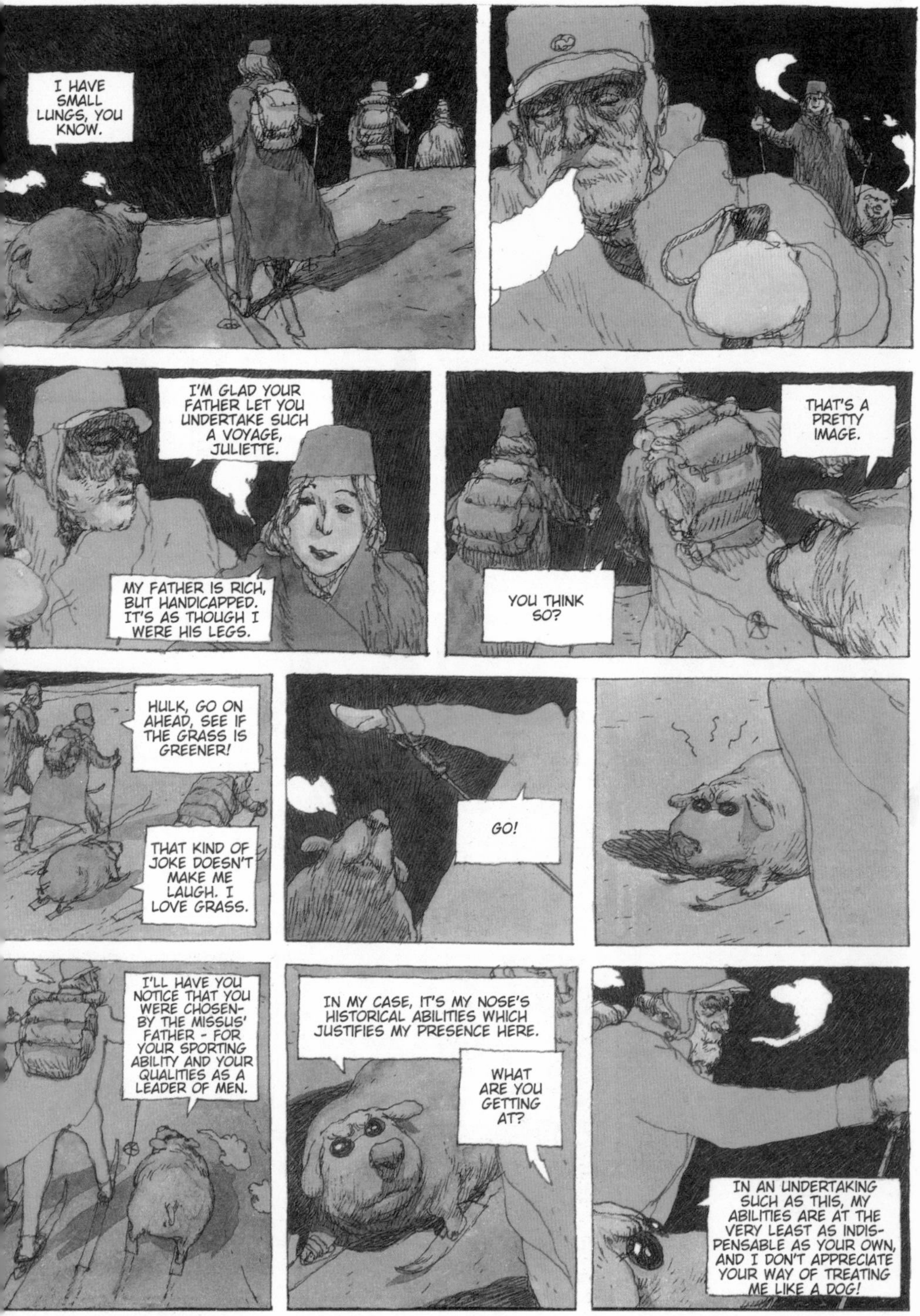
I HAVE SMALL LUNGS, YOU KNOW.
I'M GLAD YOUR FATHER LET YOU UNDERTAKE SUCH A VOYAGE, JULIETTE.
MY FATHER IS RICH, BUT HANDICAPPED. IT'S AS THOUGH I WERE HIS LEGS.
THAT'S A PRETTY IMAGE.
YOU THINK SO?
HULK, GO ON AHEAD, SEE IF THE GRASS IS GREENER!
THAT KIND OF JOKE DOESN'T MAKE ME LAUGH. I LOVE GRASS.
GO!
I'LL HAVE YOU NOTICE THAT YOU WERE CHOSEN- BY THE MISSUS' FATHER - FOR YOUR SPORTING ABILITY AND YOUR QUALITIES AS A LEADER OF MEN.
IN MY CASE, IT'S MY NOSE'S HISTORICAL ABILITIES WHICH JUSTIFIES MY PRESENCE HERE.
WHAT ARE YOU GETTING AT?
IN AN UNDERTAKING SUCH AS THIS, MY ABILITIES ARE AT THE VERY LEAST AS INDIS- PENSABLE AS YOUR OWN, AND I DON'T APPRECIATE YOUR WAY OF TREATING ME LIKE A DOG!

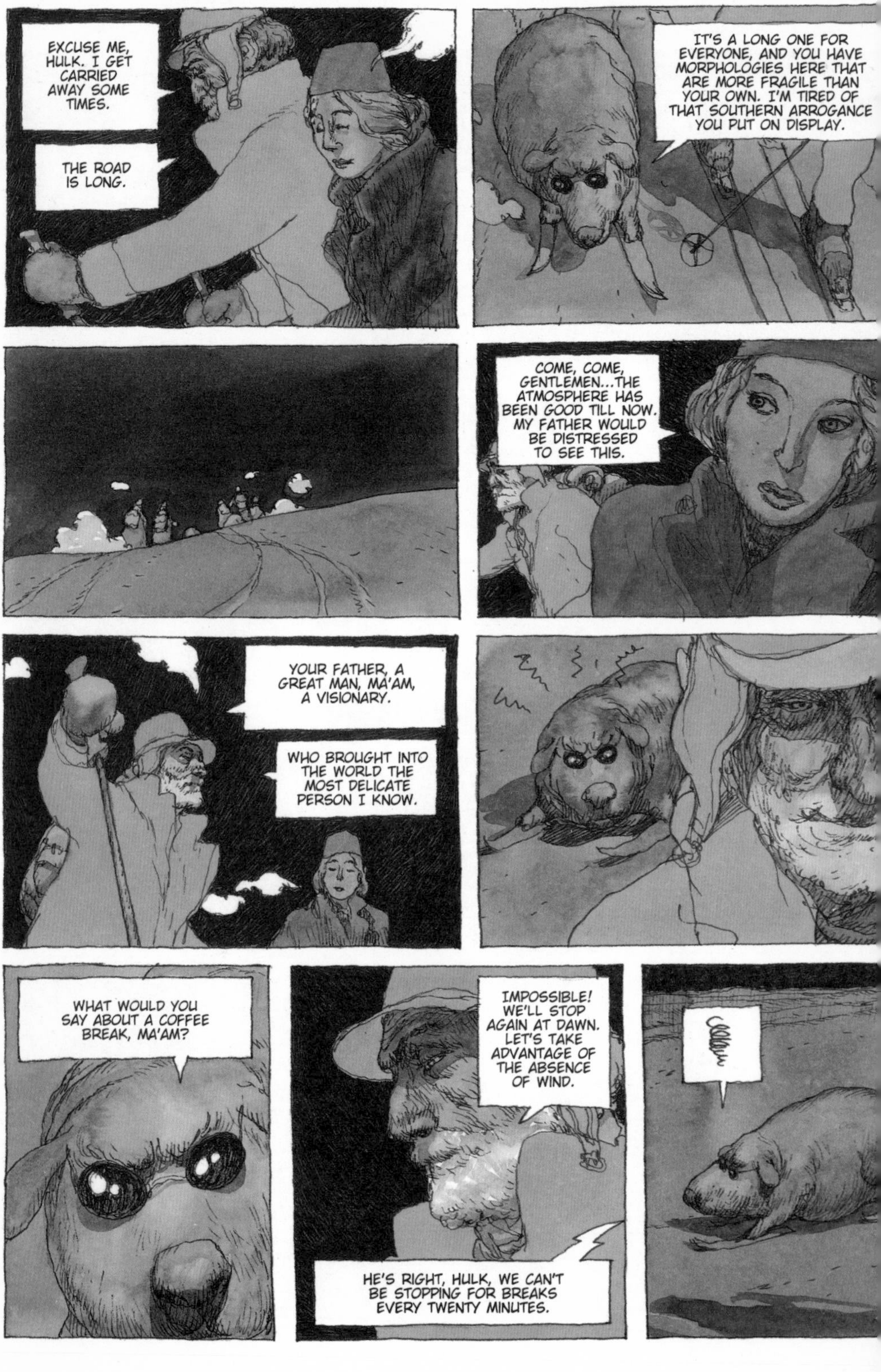
EXCUSE ME, HULK. I GET CARRIED AWAY SOME TIMES.
THE ROAD IS LONG.
IT'S A LONG ONE FOR EVERYONE, AND YOU HAVE MORPHOLOGIES HERE THAT ARE MORE FRAGILE THAN YOUR OWN. I'M TIRED OF THAT SOUTHERN ARROGANCE YOU PUT ON DISPLAY.
COME, COME, GENTLEMEN... THE ATMOSPHERE HAS BEEN GOOD TILL NOW. MY FATHER WOULD BE DISTRESSED TO SEE THIS.
YOUR FATHER, A GREAT MAN, MA'AM, A VISIONARY.
WHO BROUGHT INTO THE WORLD THE MOST DELICATE PERSON I KNOW.
WHAT WOULD YOU SAY ABOUT A COFFEE BREAK, MA'AM?
IMPOSSIBLE! WE'LL STOP AGAIN AT DAWN. LET'S TAKE ADVANTAGE OF THE ABSENCE OF WIND.
HE'S RIGHT, HULK, WE CAN'T BE STOPPING FOR BREAKS EVERY TWENTY MINUTES.

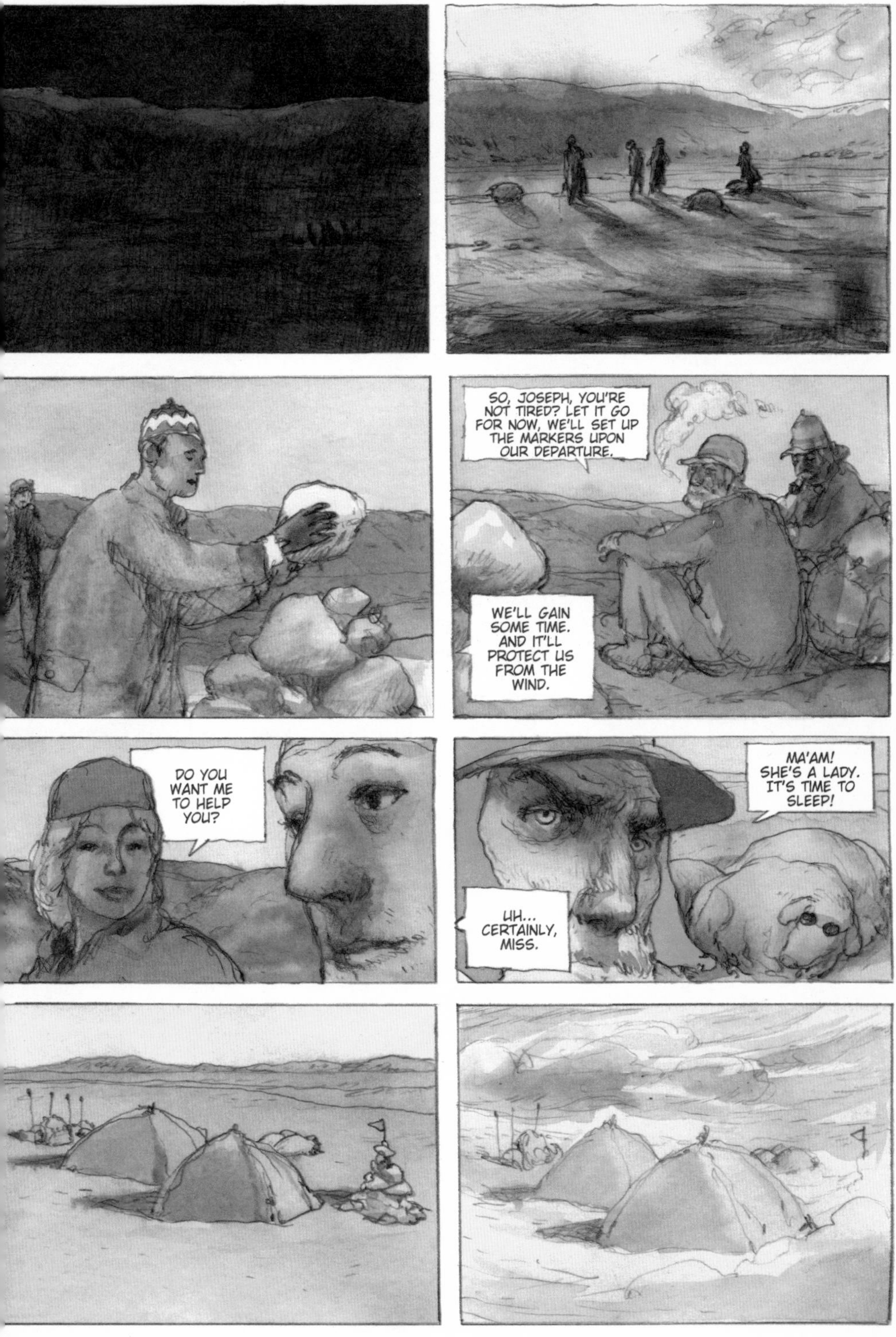
SO, JOSEPH, YOU'RE NOT TIRED? LET IT GO FOR NOW, WE'LL SET UP THE MARKERS UPON OUR DEPARTURE.
WE'LL GAIN SOME TIME. AND IT'LL PROTECT US FROM THE WIND.
DO YOU WANT ME TO HELP YOU?
MA'AM! SHE'S A LADY. IT'S TIME TO SLEEP!
UH... CERTAINLY, MISS.

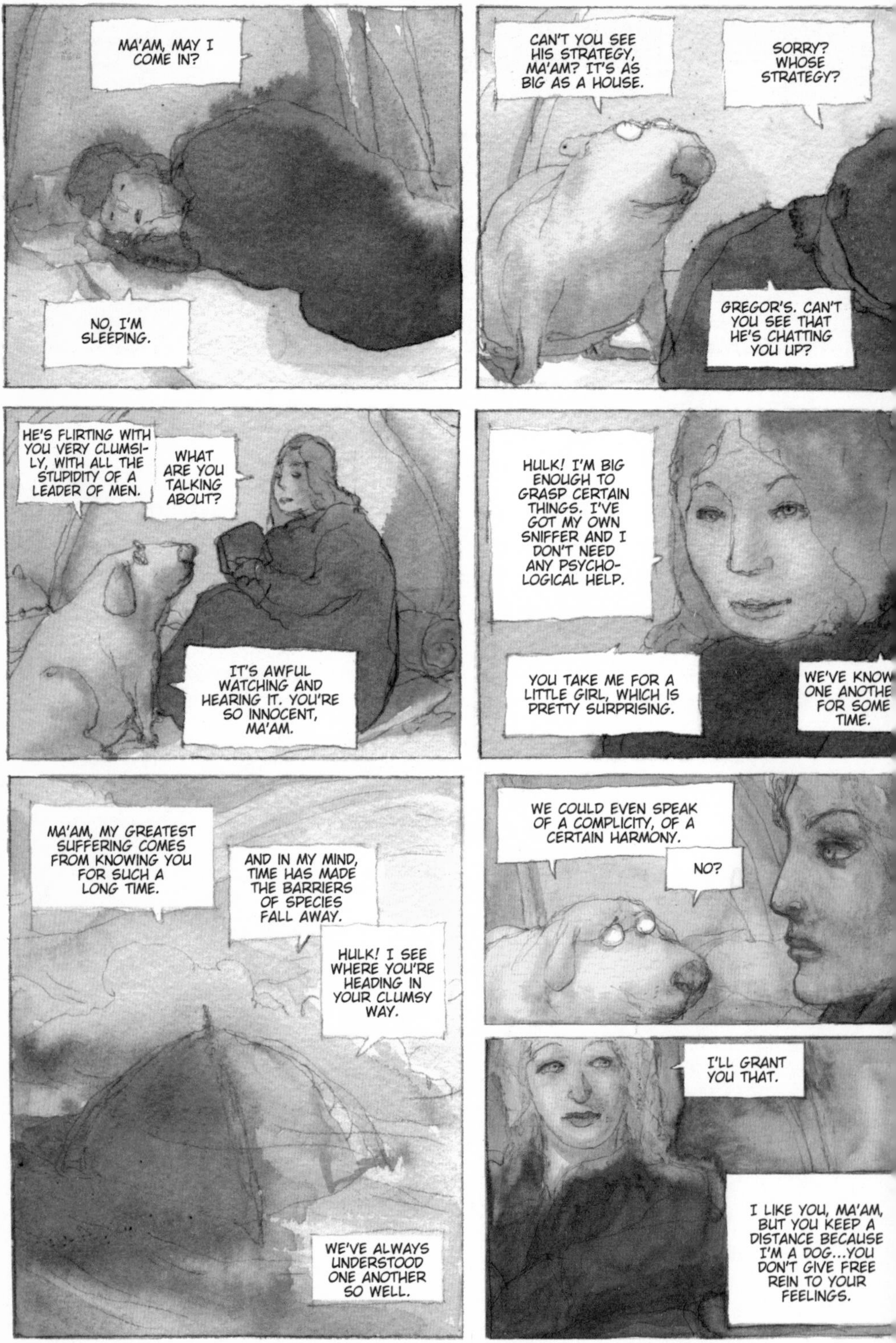
MA'AM, MAY I COME IN?
NO, I'M SLEEPING.
CAN'T YOU SEE HIS STRATEGY, MA'AM? IT'S AS BIG AS A HOUSE.
SORRY? WHOSE STRATEGY?
GREGOR'S. CAN'T YOU SEE THAT HE'S CHATTING YOU UP?
HE'S FLIRTING WITH YOU VERY CLUMSI-LY, WITH ALL THE STUPIDITY OF A LEADER OF MEN.
WHAT ARE YOU TALKING ABOUT?
IT'S AWFUL WATCHING AND HEARING IT. YOU'RE SO INNOCENT, MA'AM.
HULK! I'M BIG ENOUGH TO GRASP CERTAIN THINGS. I'VE GOT MY OWN SNIFFER AND I DON'T NEED ANY PSYCHO-LOGICAL HELP.
YOU TAKE ME FOR A LITTLE GIRL, WHICH IS PRETTY SURPRISING.
WE'VE KNOW ONE ANOTHE FOR SOME TIME.
MA'AM, MY GREATEST SUFFERING COMES FROM KNOWING YOU FOR SUCH A LONG TIME.
AND IN MY MIND, TIME HAS MADE THE BARRIERS OF SPECIES FALL AWAY.
HULK! I SEE WHERE YOU'RE HEADING IN YOUR CLUMSY WAY.
WE'VE ALWAYS UNDERSTOOD ONE ANOTHER SO WELL.
WE COULD EVEN SPEAK OF A COMPLICITY, OF A CERTAIN HARMONY.
NO?
I'LL GRANT YOU THAT.
I LIKE YOU, MA'AM, BUT YOU KEEP A DISTANCE BECAUSE I'M A DOG…YOU DON'T GIVE FREE REIN TO YOUR FEELINGS.

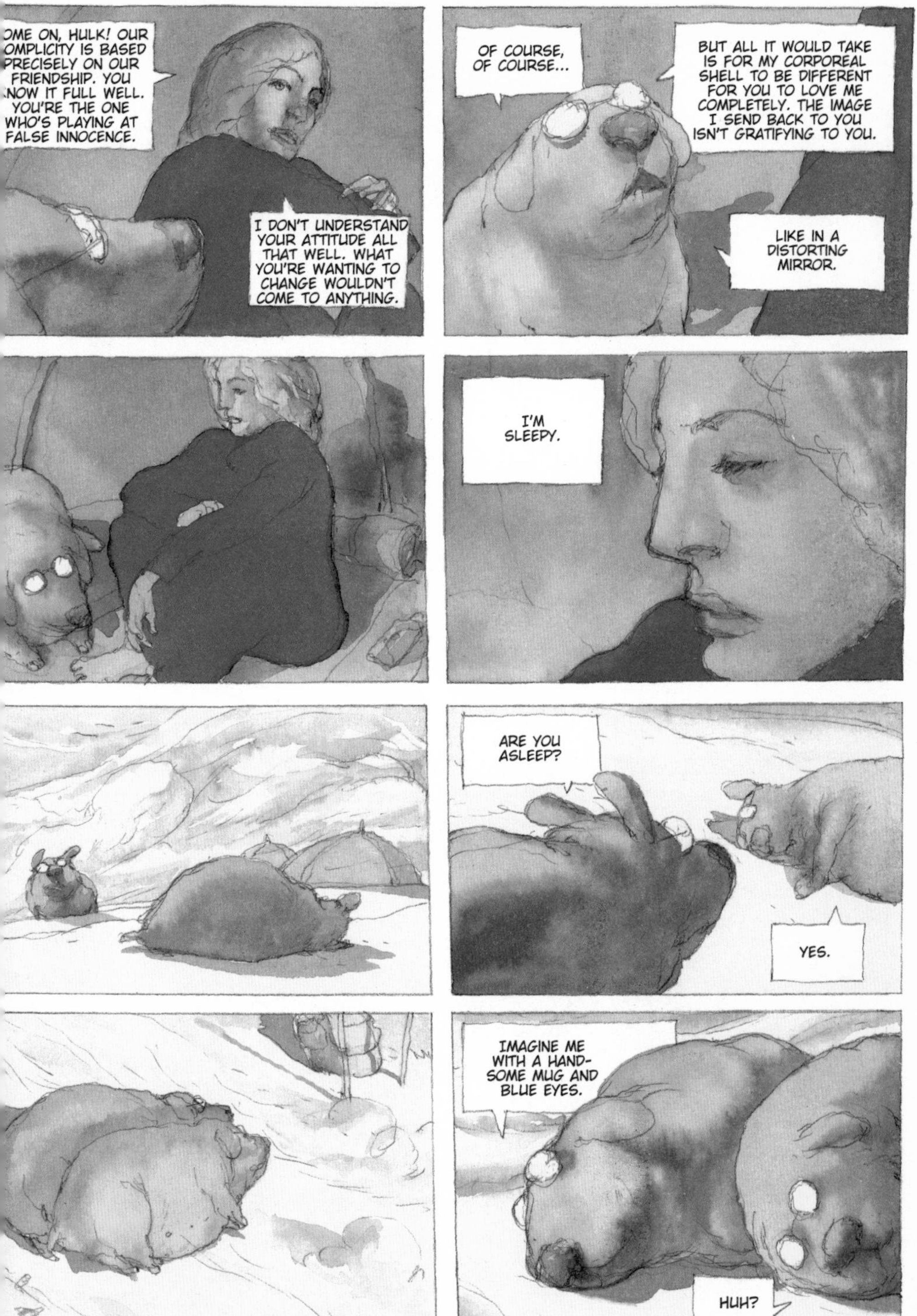
OME ON, HULK! OUR OMPLICITY IS BASED PRECISELY ON OUR FRIENDSHIP. YOU NOW IT FULL WELL. YOU'RE THE ONE WHO'S PLAYING AT FALSE INNOCENCE.
I DON'T UNDERSTAND YOUR ATTITUDE ALL THAT WELL. WHAT YOU'RE WANTING TO CHANGE WOULDN'T COME TO ANYTHING.
OF COURSE, OF COURSE...
BUT ALL IT WOULD TAKE IS FOR MY CORPOREAL SHELL TO BE DIFFERENT FOR YOU TO LOVE ME COMPLETELY. THE IMAGE I SEND BACK TO YOU ISN'T GRATIFYING TO YOU.
LIKE IN A DISTORTING MIRROR.
I'M SLEEPY.
ARE YOU ASLEEP?
YES.
IMAGINE ME WITH A HAND-SOME MUG AND BLUE EYES.
HUH?

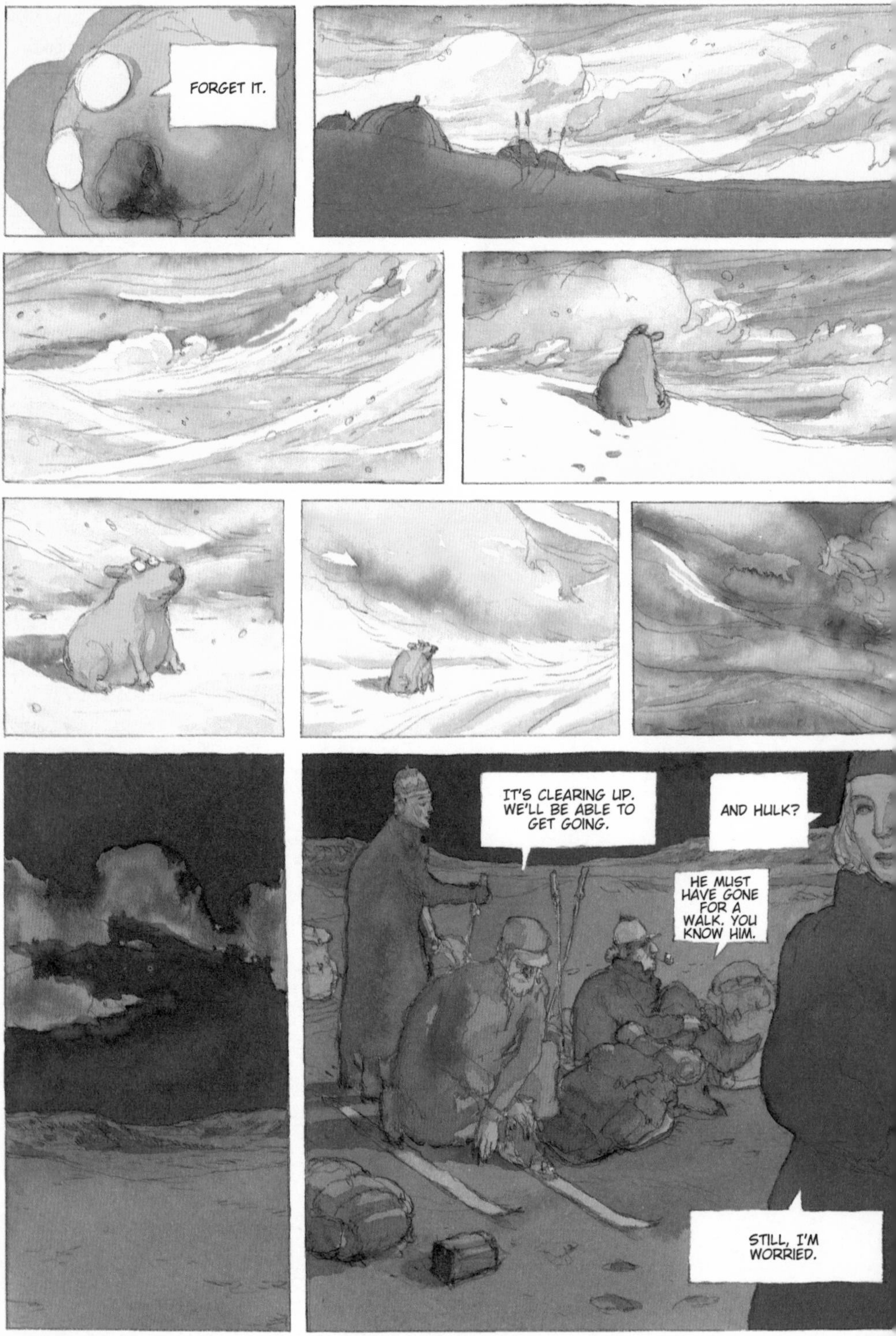
FORGET IT.
IT'S CLEARING UP. WE'LL BE ABLE TO GET GOING.
AND HULK?
HE MUST HAVE GONE FOR A WALK. YOU KNOW HIM.
STILL, I'M WORRIED.

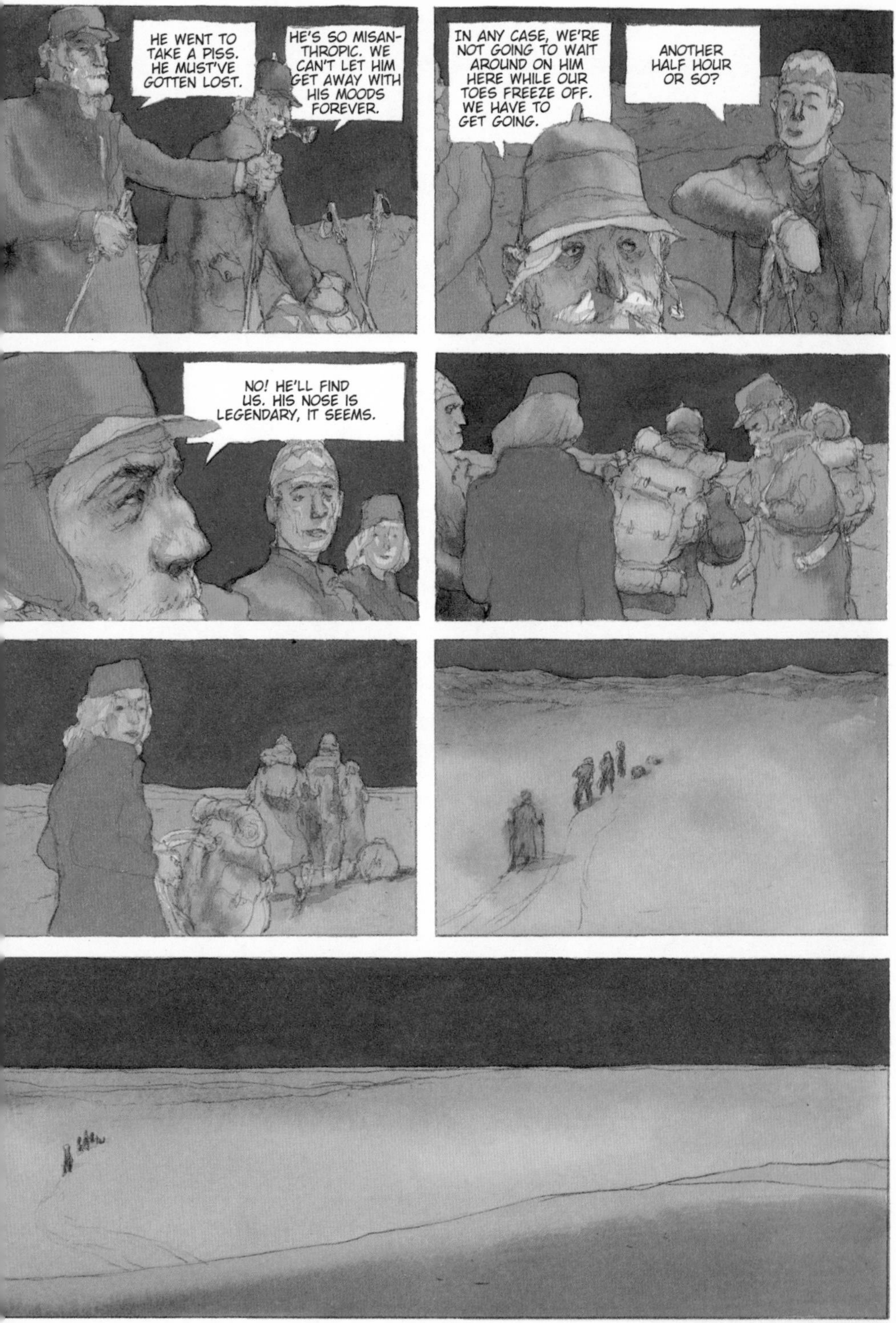
HE WENT TO TAKE A PISS. HE MUST'VE GOTTEN LOST.
HE'S SO MISANTHROPIC. WE CAN'T LET HIM GET AWAY WITH HIS MOODS FOREVER.
IN ANY CASE, WE'RE NOT GOING TO WAIT AROUND ON HIM HERE WHILE OUR TOES FREEZE OFF. WE HAVE TO GET GOING.
ANOTHER HALF HOUR OR SO?
NO! HE'LL FIND US. HIS NOSE IS LEGENDARY, IT SEEMS.

ZZZZZ
RRRZZZ
RZZ... HM!
NIGHT ALREADY?
FLAP FLAP FLAP!
SNFF SNFF
THE SNOW COVERED OVER MY TRACKS.
SNFF SNFF...STILL THIS BLASTED COLD.
SNFF.
I MUST BE ALLERGIC TO SOMETHING, SNFF SNFF.

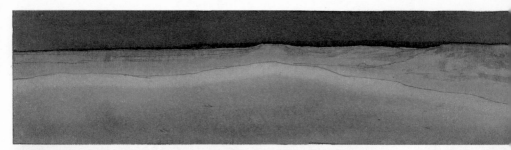

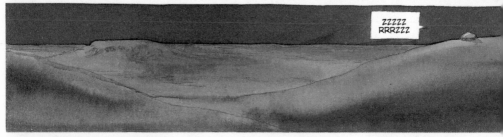

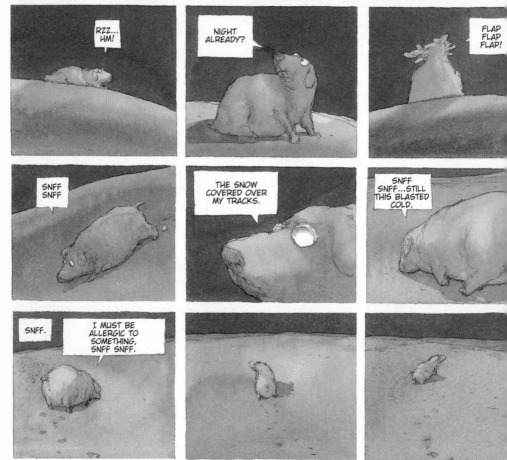

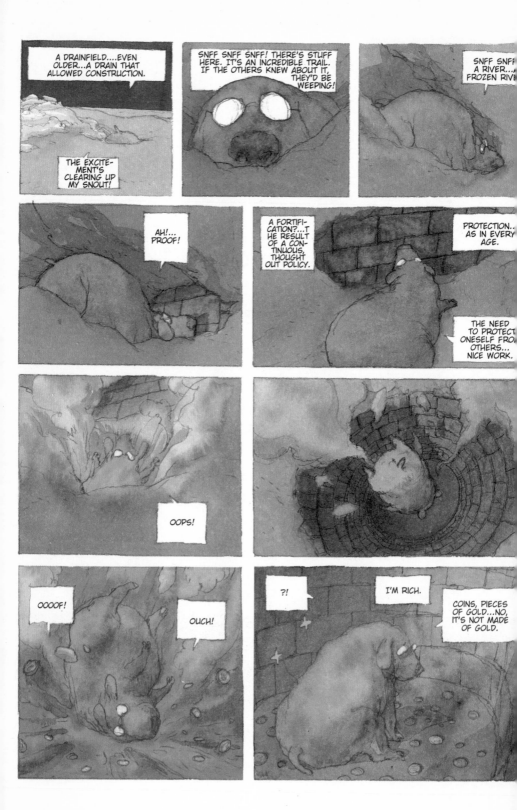

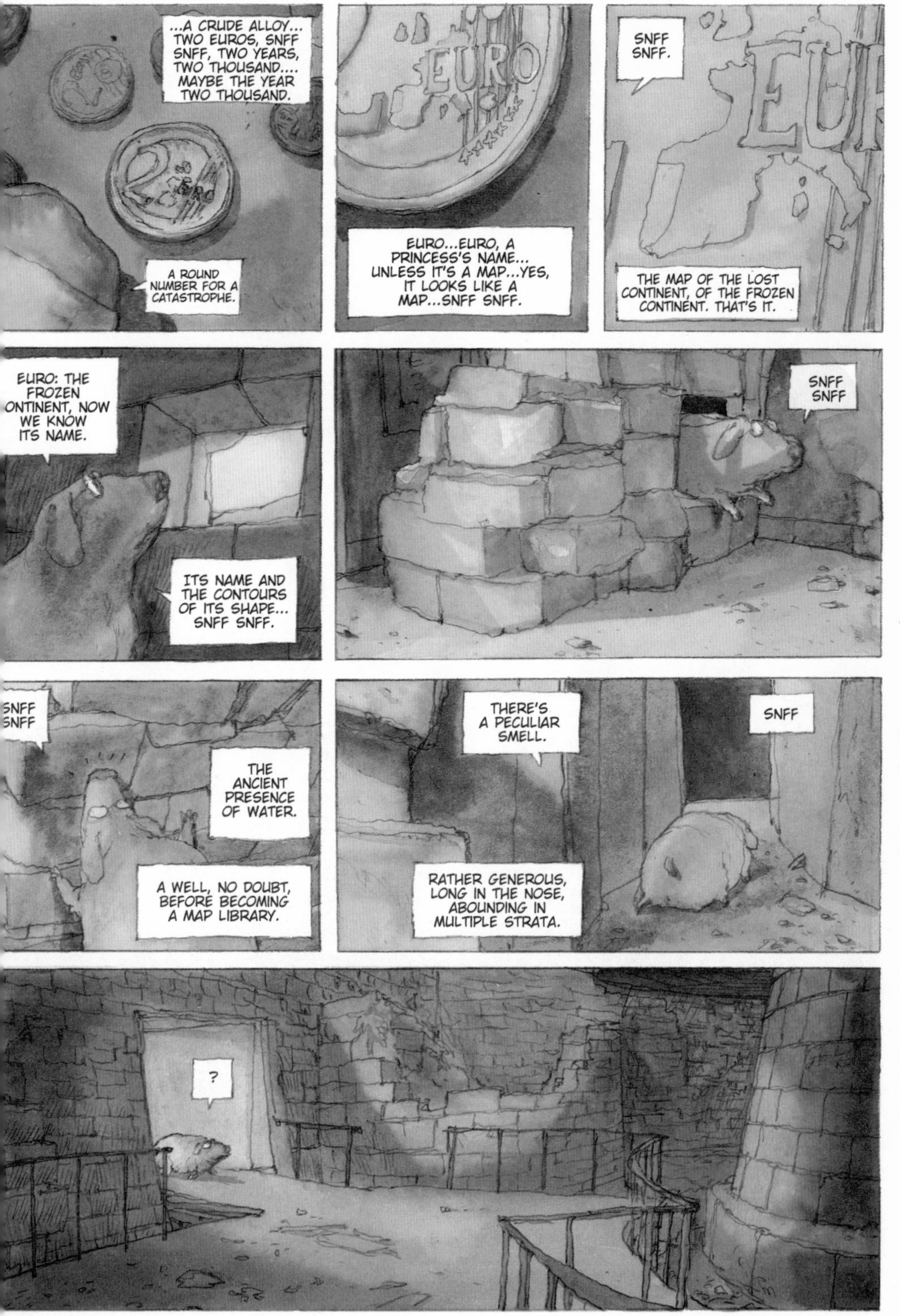
...A CRUDE ALLOY... TWO EUROS, SNFF SNFF, TWO YEARS, TWO THOUSAND.... MAYBE THE YEAR TWO THOUSAND.
A ROUND NUMBER FOR A CATASTROPHE.
EURO
EURO...EURO, A PRINCESS'S NAME... UNLESS IT'S A MAP...YES, IT LOOKS LIKE A MAP...SNFF SNFF.
SNFF SNFF.
THE MAP OF THE LOST CONTINENT, OF THE FROZEN CONTINENT. THAT'S IT.
EURO: THE FROZEN ONTINENT, NOW WE KNOW ITS NAME.
ITS NAME AND THE CONTOURS OF ITS SHAPE... SNFF SNFF.
SNFF SNFF
SNFF SNFF
THE ANCIENT PRESENCE OF WATER.
A WELL, NO DOUBT, BEFORE BECOMING A MAP LIBRARY.
THERE'S A PECULIAR SMELL.
SNFF
RATHER GENEROUS, LONG IN THE NOSE, ABOUNDING IN MULTIPLE STRATA.
?

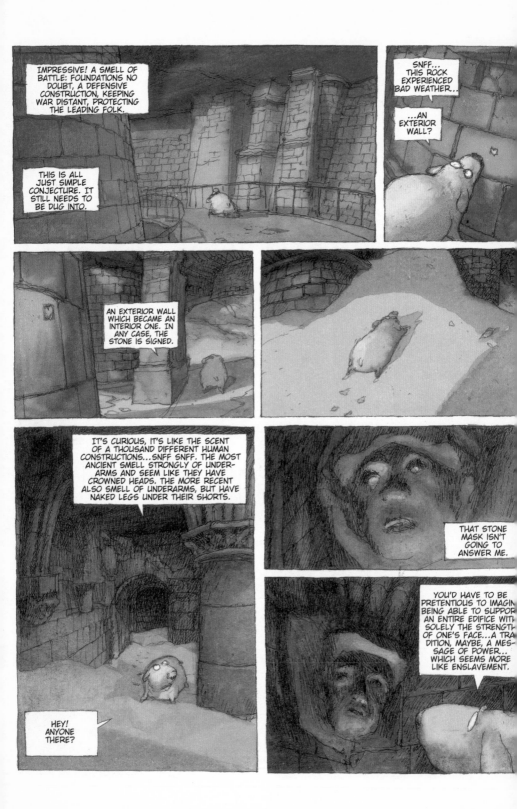

IMPRESSIVE! A SMELL OF BATTLE: FOUNDATIONS NO DOUBT, A DEFENSIVE CONSTRUCTION, KEEPING WAR DISTANT, PROTECTING THE LEADING FOLK.

THIS IS ALL JUST SIMPLE CONJECTURE. IT STILL NEEDS TO BE DUG INTO.

SNFF... THIS ROCK EXPERIENCED BAD WEATHER...

...AN EXTERIOR WALL?

AN EXTERIOR WALL WHICH BECAME AN INTERIOR ONE. IN ANY CASE, THE STONE IS SIGNED.

IT'S CURIOUS, IT'S LIKE THE SCENT OF A THOUSAND DIFFERENT HUMAN CONSTRUCTIONS...SNFF SNFF. THE MOST ANCIENT SMELL STRONGLY OF UNDER-ARMS AND SEEM LIKE THEY HAVE CROWNED HEADS. THE MORE RECENT ALSO SMELL OF UNDERARMS, BUT HAVE NAKED LEGS UNDER THEIR SHORTS.

THAT STONE MASK ISN'T GOING TO ANSWER ME.

YOU'D HAVE TO BE PRETENTIOUS TO IMAGIN BEING ABLE TO SUPPOR AN ENTIRE EDIFICE WIT SOLELY THE STRENGTI OF ONE'S FACE...A TRA DITION, MAYBE, A MES-SAGE OF POWER... WHICH SEEMS MORE LIKE ENSLAVEMENT.

HEY! ANYONE THERE?

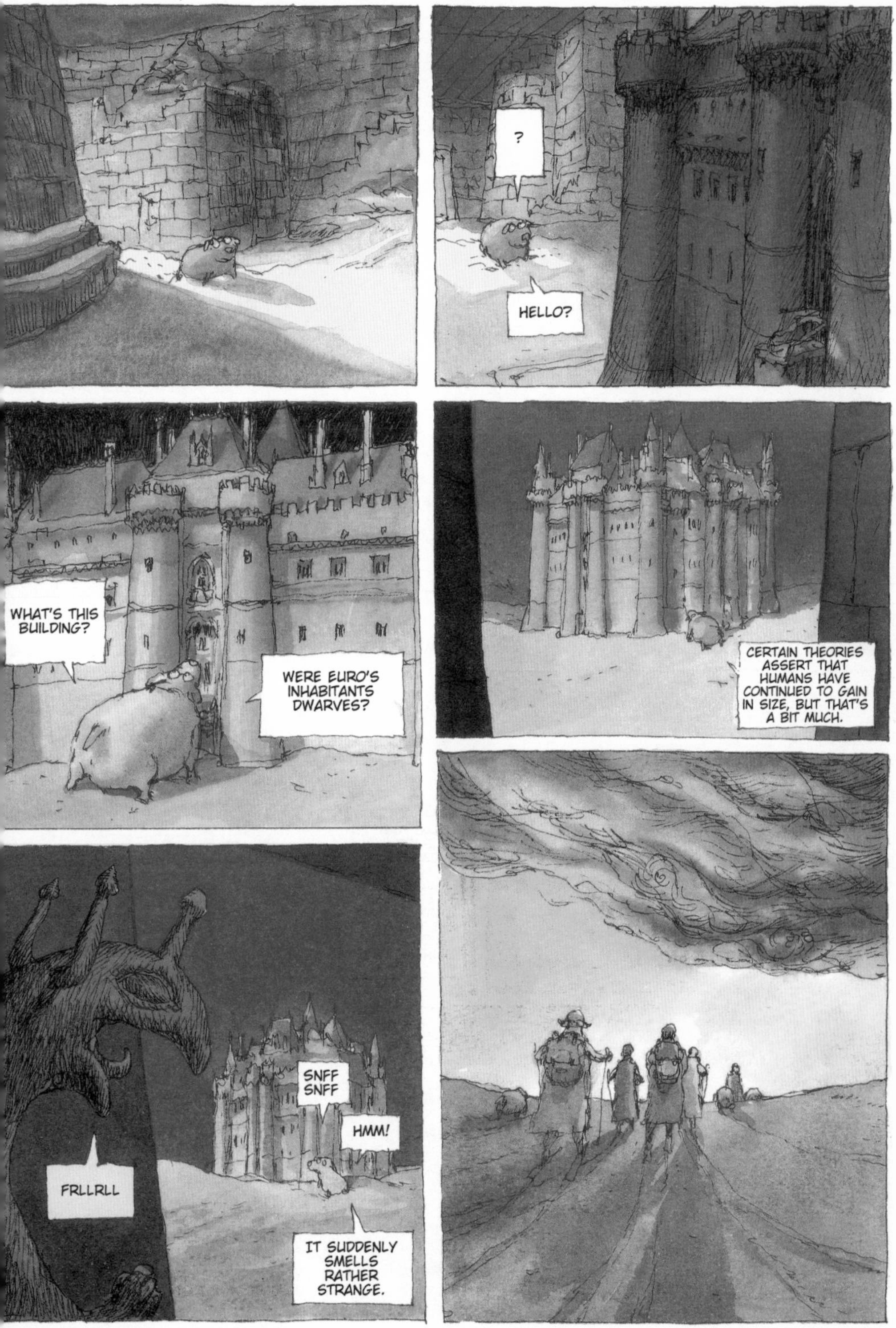
?
HELLO?
WHAT'S THIS BUILDING?
WERE EURO'S INHABITANTS DWARVES?
CERTAIN THEORIES ASSERT THAT HUMANS HAVE CONTINUED TO GAIN IN SIZE, BUT THAT'S A BIT MUCH.
FRLLRLL
SNFF SNFF
HMM!
IT SUDDENLY SMELLS RATHER STRANGE.

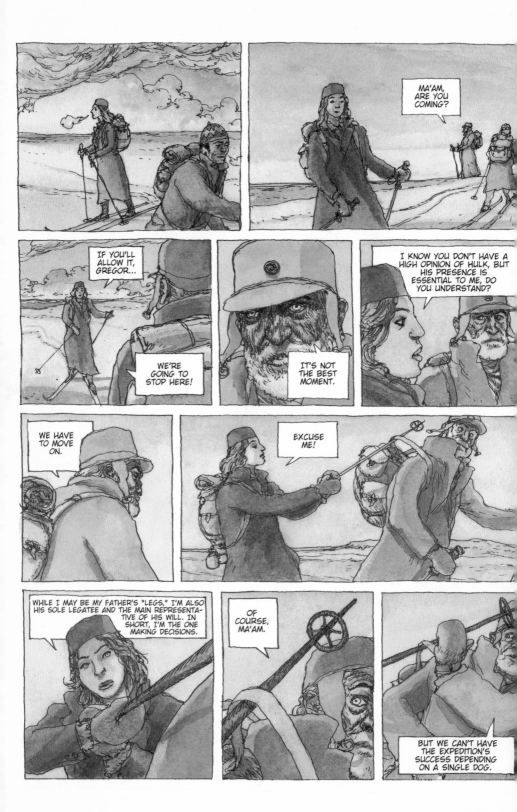

29

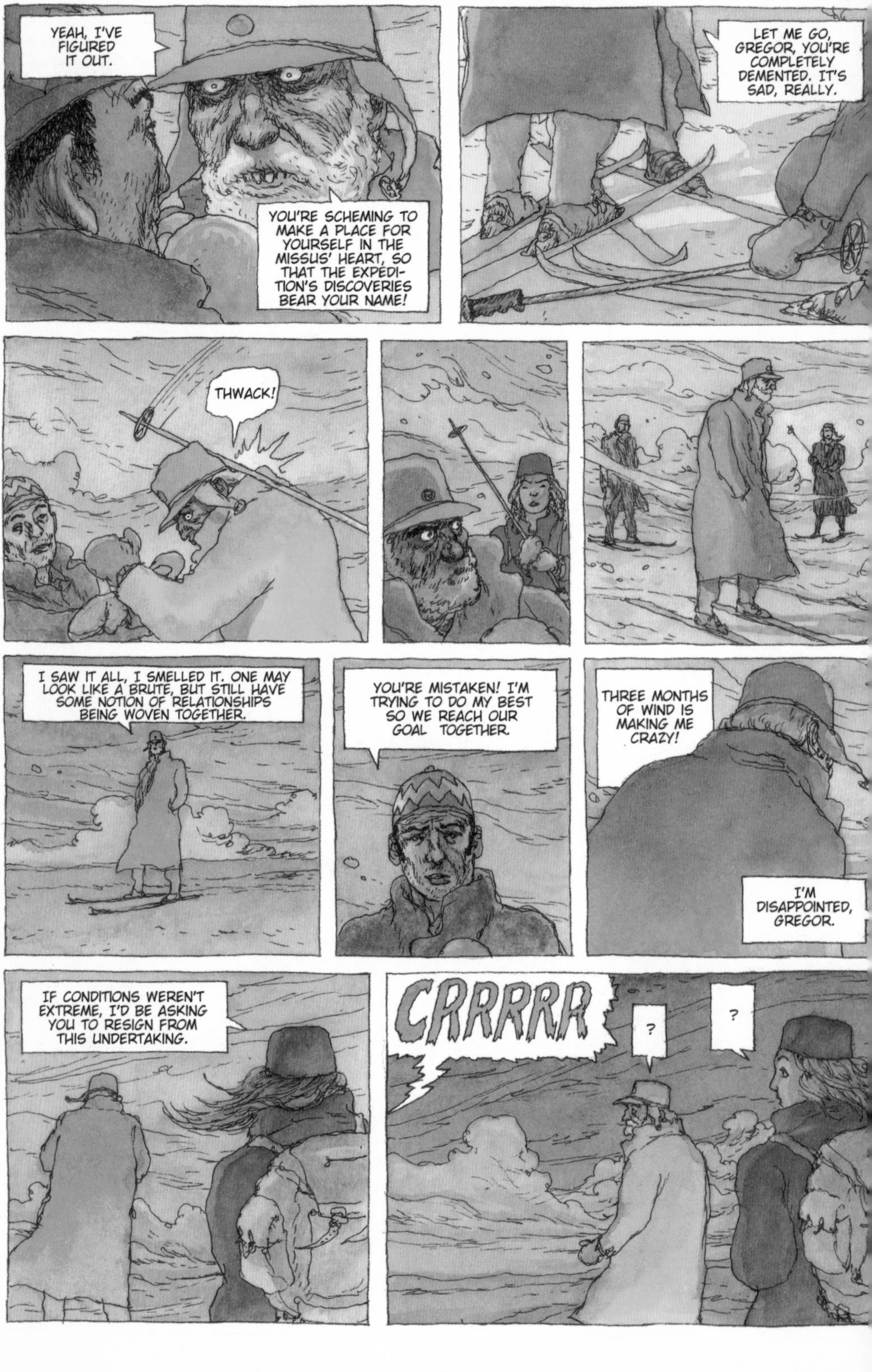
YEAH, I'VE FIGURED IT OUT.
YOU'RE SCHEMING TO MAKE A PLACE FOR YOURSELF IN THE MISSUS' HEART, SO THAT THE EXPEDITION'S DISCOVERIES BEAR YOUR NAME!
LET ME GO, GREGOR, YOU'RE COMPLETELY DEMENTED. IT'S SAD, REALLY.
THWACK!
I SAW IT ALL, I SMELLED IT. ONE MAY LOOK LIKE A BRUTE, BUT STILL HAVE SOME NOTION OF RELATIONSHIPS BEING WOVEN TOGETHER.
YOU'RE MISTAKEN! I'M TRYING TO DO MY BEST SO WE REACH OUR GOAL TOGETHER.
THREE MONTHS OF WIND IS MAKING ME CRAZY!
I'M DISAPPOINTED, GREGOR.
IF CONDITIONS WEREN'T EXTREME, I'D BE ASKING YOU TO RESIGN FROM THIS UNDERTAKING.
CRRRRR
?
?

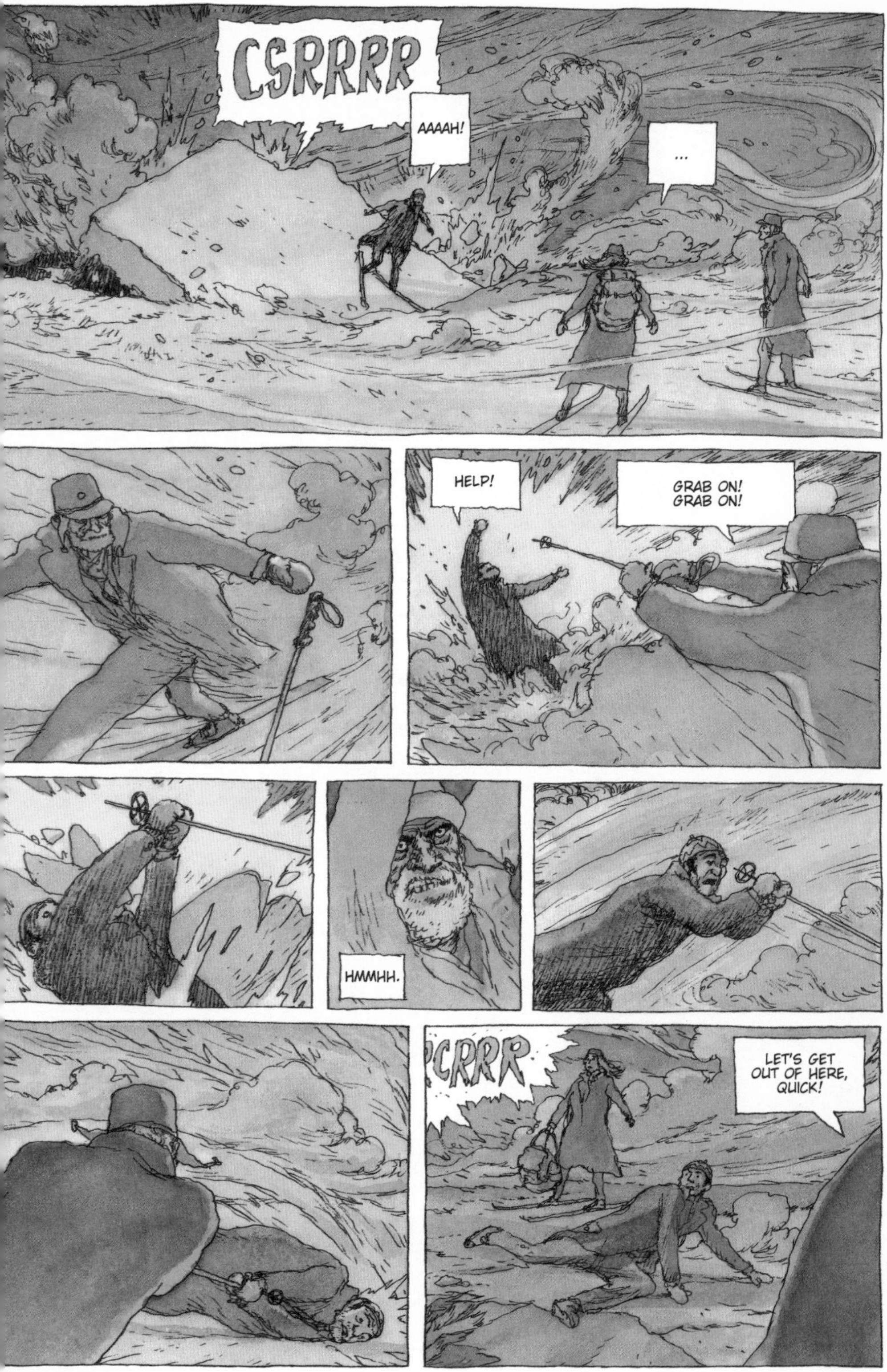
CSRRRR
AAAAH!
...
HELP!
GRAB ON! GRAB ON!
HMMHH.
CRRR
LET'S GET OUT OF HERE, QUICK!

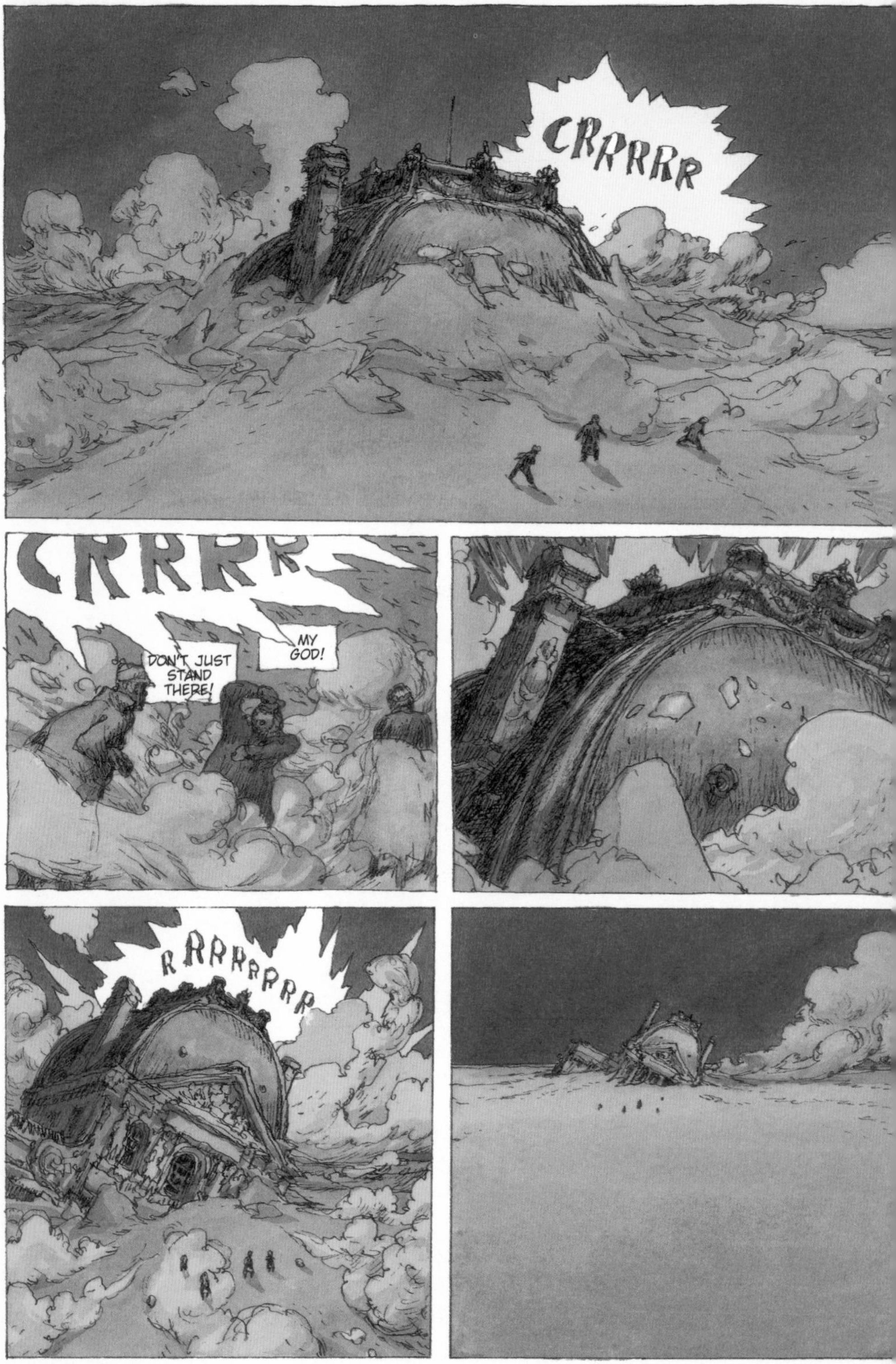
CRRRRRR
CRRRR
DON'T JUST STAND THERE!
MY GOD!
RRRRRRRRR

35

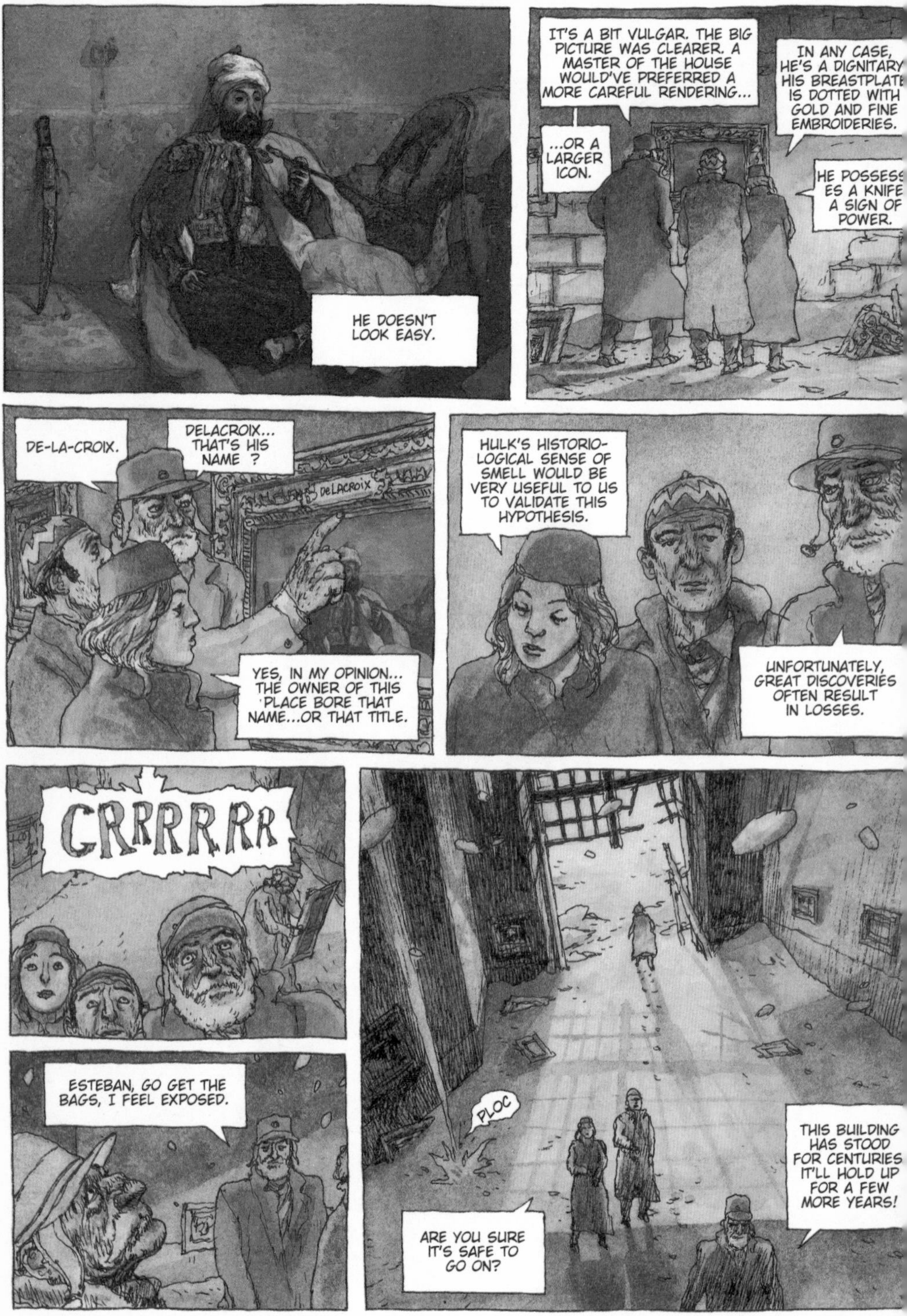
HE DOESN'T LOOK EASY.
IT'S A BIT VULGAR. THE BIG PICTURE WAS CLEARER. A MASTER OF THE HOUSE WOULD'VE PREFERRED A MORE CAREFUL RENDERING...
...OR A LARGER ICON.
IN ANY CASE, HE'S A DIGNITARY HIS BREASTPLATE IS DOTTED WITH GOLD AND FINE EMBROIDERIES.
HE POSSESSES A KNIFE A SIGN OF POWER.
DE-LA-CROIX.
DELACROIX... THAT'S HIS NAME ?
DeLACROIX
YES, IN MY OPINION... THE OWNER OF THIS PLACE BORE THAT NAME...OR THAT TITLE.
HULK'S HISTORIO-LOGICAL SENSE OF SMELL WOULD BE VERY USEFUL TO US TO VALIDATE THIS HYPOTHESIS.
UNFORTUNATELY, GREAT DISCOVERIES OFTEN RESULT IN LOSSES.
CRRRRRR
ESTEBAN, GO GET THE BAGS, I FEEL EXPOSED.
PLOC
ARE YOU SURE IT'S SAFE TO GO ON?
THIS BUILDING HAS STOOD FOR CENTURIES IT'LL HOLD UP FOR A FEW MORE YEARS!

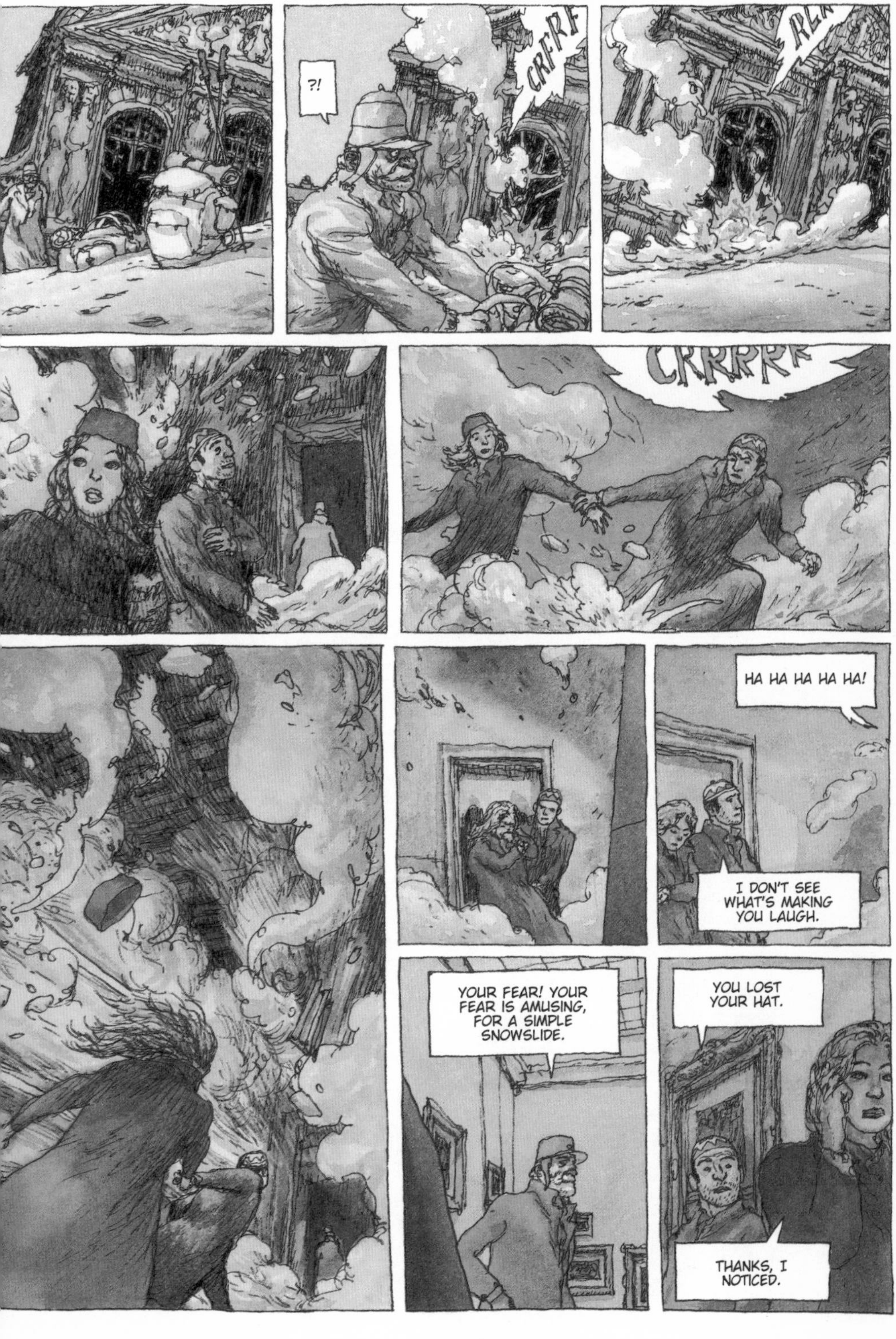
?!
CRFRF
RFR
CRRRRR
HA HA HA HA HA!
I DON'T SEE WHAT'S MAKING YOU LAUGH.
YOUR FEAR! YOUR FEAR IS AMUSING, FOR A SIMPLE SNOWSLIDE.
YOU LOST YOUR HAT.
THANKS, I NOTICED.

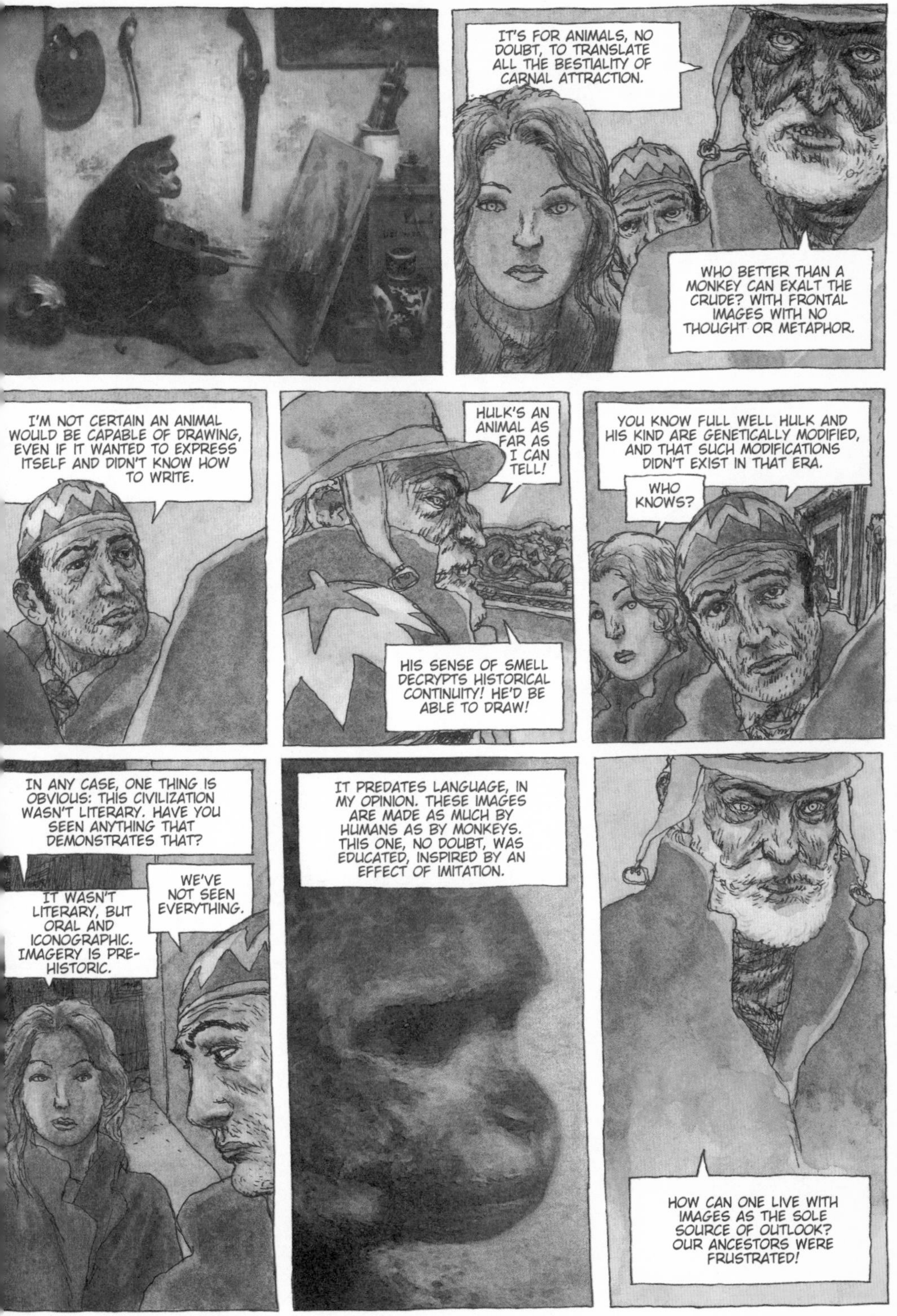

IT'S FOR ANIMALS, NO DOUBT, TO TRANSLATE ALL THE BESTIALITY OF CARNAL ATTRACTION.
WHO BETTER THAN A MONKEY CAN EXALT THE CRUDE? WITH FRONTAL IMAGES WITH NO THOUGHT OR METAPHOR.
I'M NOT CERTAIN AN ANIMAL WOULD BE CAPABLE OF DRAWING, EVEN IF IT WANTED TO EXPRESS ITSELF AND DIDN'T KNOW HOW TO WRITE.
HULK'S AN ANIMAL AS FAR AS I CAN TELL!
HIS SENSE OF SMELL DECRYPTS HISTORICAL CONTINUITY! HE'D BE ABLE TO DRAW!
YOU KNOW FULL WELL HULK AND HIS KIND ARE GENETICALLY MODIFIED, AND THAT SUCH MODIFICATIONS DIDN'T EXIST IN THAT ERA.
WHO KNOWS?
IN ANY CASE, ONE THING IS OBVIOUS: THIS CIVILIZATION WASN'T LITERARY. HAVE YOU SEEN ANYTHING THAT DEMONSTRATES THAT?
WE'VE NOT SEEN EVERYTHING.
IT WASN'T LITERARY, BUT ORAL AND ICONOGRAPHIC. IMAGERY IS PRE-HISTORIC.
IT PREDATES LANGUAGE, IN MY OPINION. THESE IMAGES ARE MADE AS MUCH BY HUMANS AS BY MONKEYS. THIS ONE, NO DOUBT, WAS EDUCATED, INSPIRED BY AN EFFECT OF IMITATION.
HOW CAN ONE LIVE WITH IMAGES AS THE SOLE SOURCE OF OUTLOOK? OUR ANCESTORS WERE FRUSTRATED!

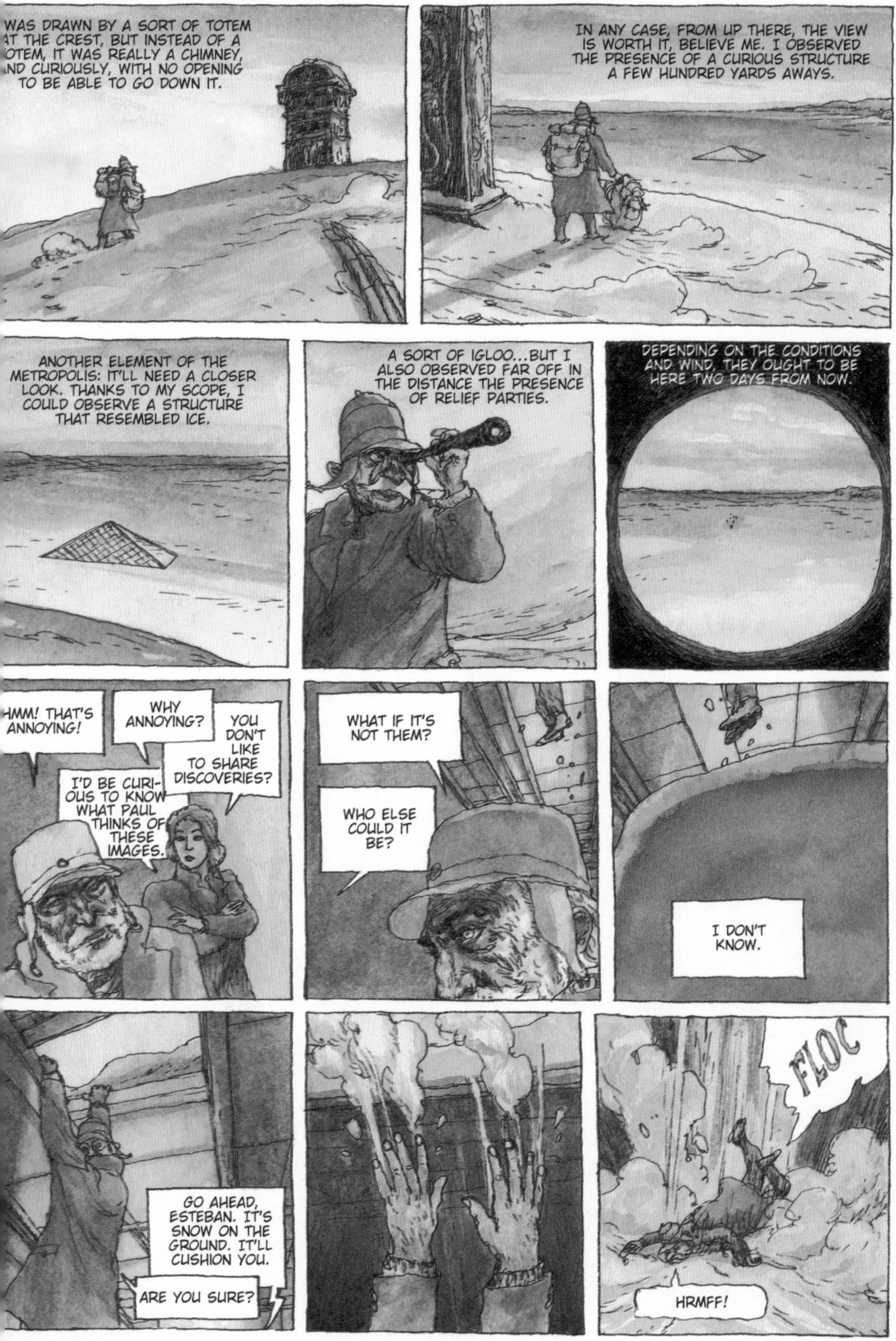
WAS DRAWN BY A SORT OF TOTEM AT THE CREST, BUT INSTEAD OF A TOTEM, IT WAS REALLY A CHIMNEY, AND CURIOUSLY, WITH NO OPENING TO BE ABLE TO GO DOWN IT.
IN ANY CASE, FROM UP THERE, THE VIEW IS WORTH IT, BELIEVE ME. I OBSERVED THE PRESENCE OF A CURIOUS STRUCTURE A FEW HUNDRED YARDS AWAYS.
ANOTHER ELEMENT OF THE METROPOLIS: IT'LL NEED A CLOSER LOOK. THANKS TO MY SCOPE, I COULD OBSERVE A STRUCTURE THAT RESEMBLED ICE.
A SORT OF IGLOO...BUT I ALSO OBSERVED FAR OFF IN THE DISTANCE THE PRESENCE OF RELIEF PARTIES.
DEPENDING ON THE CONDITIONS AND WIND, THEY OUGHT TO BE HERE TWO DAYS FROM NOW.
HMM! THAT'S ANNOYING!
WHY ANNOYING?
YOU DON'T LIKE TO SHARE DISCOVERIES?
I'D BE CURIOUS TO KNOW WHAT PAUL THINKS OF THESE IMAGES.
WHAT IF IT'S NOT THEM?
WHO ELSE COULD IT BE?
I DON'T KNOW.
GO AHEAD, ESTEBAN. IT'S SNOW ON THE GROUND. IT'LL CUSHION YOU.
ARE YOU SURE?
FLOC
HRMFF!

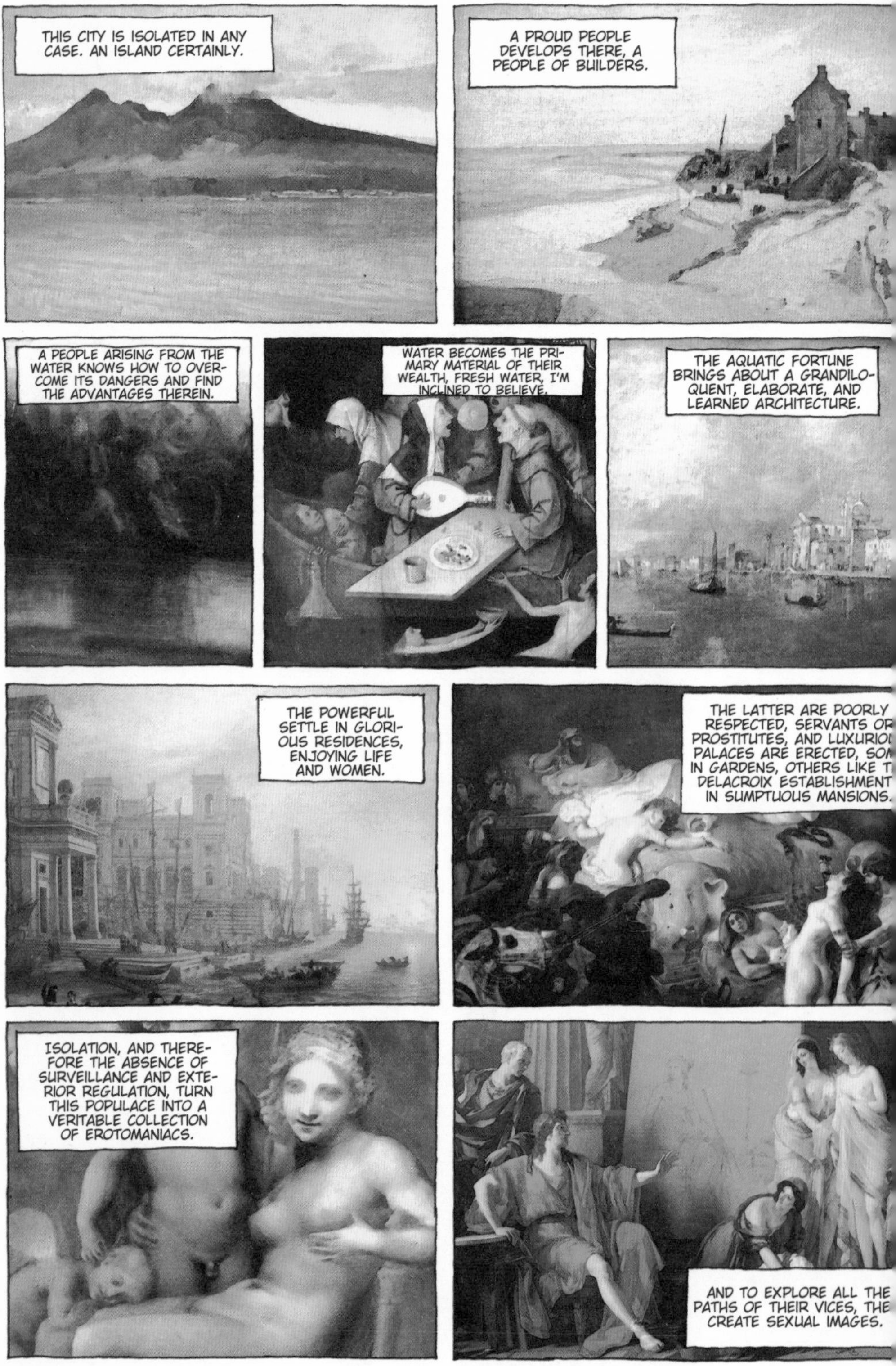
THIS CITY IS ISOLATED IN ANY CASE. AN ISLAND CERTAINLY.
A PROUD PEOPLE DEVELOPS THERE, A PEOPLE OF BUILDERS.
A PEOPLE ARISING FROM THE WATER KNOWS HOW TO OVER-COME ITS DANGERS AND FIND THE ADVANTAGES THEREIN.
WATER BECOMES THE PRI-MARY MATERIAL OF THEIR WEALTH, FRESH WATER, I'M INCLINED TO BELIEVE.
THE AQUATIC FORTUNE BRINGS ABOUT A GRANDILO-QUENT, ELABORATE, AND LEARNED ARCHITECTURE.
THE POWERFUL SETTLE IN GLORI-OUS RESIDENCES, ENJOYING LIFE AND WOMEN.
THE LATTER ARE POORLY RESPECTED, SERVANTS OR PROSTITUTES, AND LUXURIO PALACES ARE ERECTED, SOM IN GARDENS, OTHERS LIKE T DELACROIX ESTABLISHMENT IN SUMPTUOUS MANSIONS.
ISOLATION, AND THERE-FORE THE ABSENCE OF SURVEILLANCE AND EXTE-RIOR REGULATION, TURN THIS POPULACE INTO A VERITABLE COLLECTION OF EROTOMANIACS.
AND TO EXPLORE ALL THE PATHS OF THEIR VICES, THE CREATE SEXUAL IMAGES.

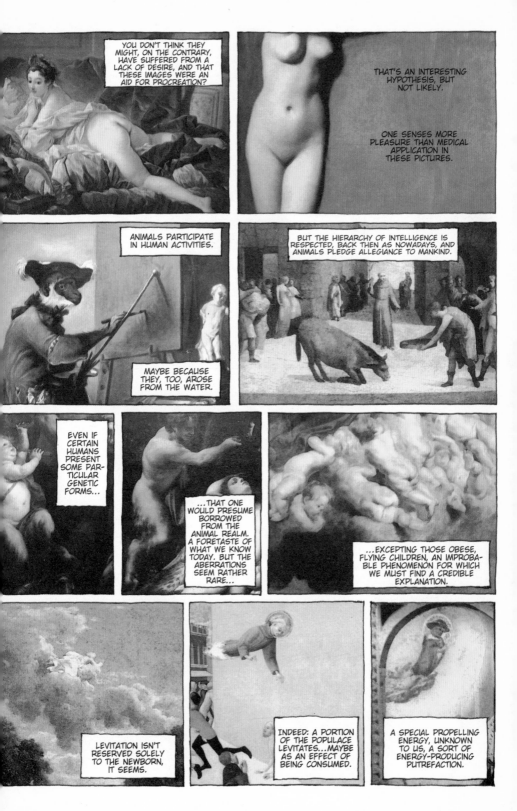

YOU DON'T THINK THEY MIGHT, ON THE CONTRARY, HAVE SUFFERED FROM A LACK OF DESIRE, AND THAT THESE IMAGES WERE AN AID FOR PROCREATION?

THAT'S AN INTERESTING HYPOTHESIS, BUT NOT LIKELY.

ONE SENSES MORE PLEASURE THAN MEDICAL APPLICATION IN THESE PICTURES.

ANIMALS PARTICIPATE IN HUMAN ACTIVITIES.

MAYBE BECAUSE THEY, TOO, AROSE FROM THE WATER.

BUT THE HIERARCHY OF INTELLIGENCE IS RESPECTED, BACK THEN AS NOWADAYS, AND ANIMALS PLEDGE ALLEGIANCE TO MANKIND.

EVEN IF CERTAIN HUMANS PRESENT SOME PARTICULAR GENETIC FORMS...

...THAT ONE WOULD PRESUME BORROWED FROM THE ANIMAL REALM. A FORETASTE OF WHAT WE KNOW TODAY. BUT THE ABERRATIONS SEEM RATHER RARE...

...EXCEPTING THOSE OBESE, FLYING CHILDREN, AN IMPROBABLE PHENOMENON FOR WHICH WE MUST FIND A CREDIBLE EXPLANATION.

LEVITATION ISN'T RESERVED SOLELY TO THE NEWBORN, IT SEEMS.

INDEED: A PORTION OF THE POPULACE LEVITATES...MAYBE AS AN EFFECT OF BEING CONSUMED.

A SPECIAL PROPELLING ENERGY, UNKNOWN TO US, A SORT OF ENERGY-PRODUCING PUTREFACTION.

45

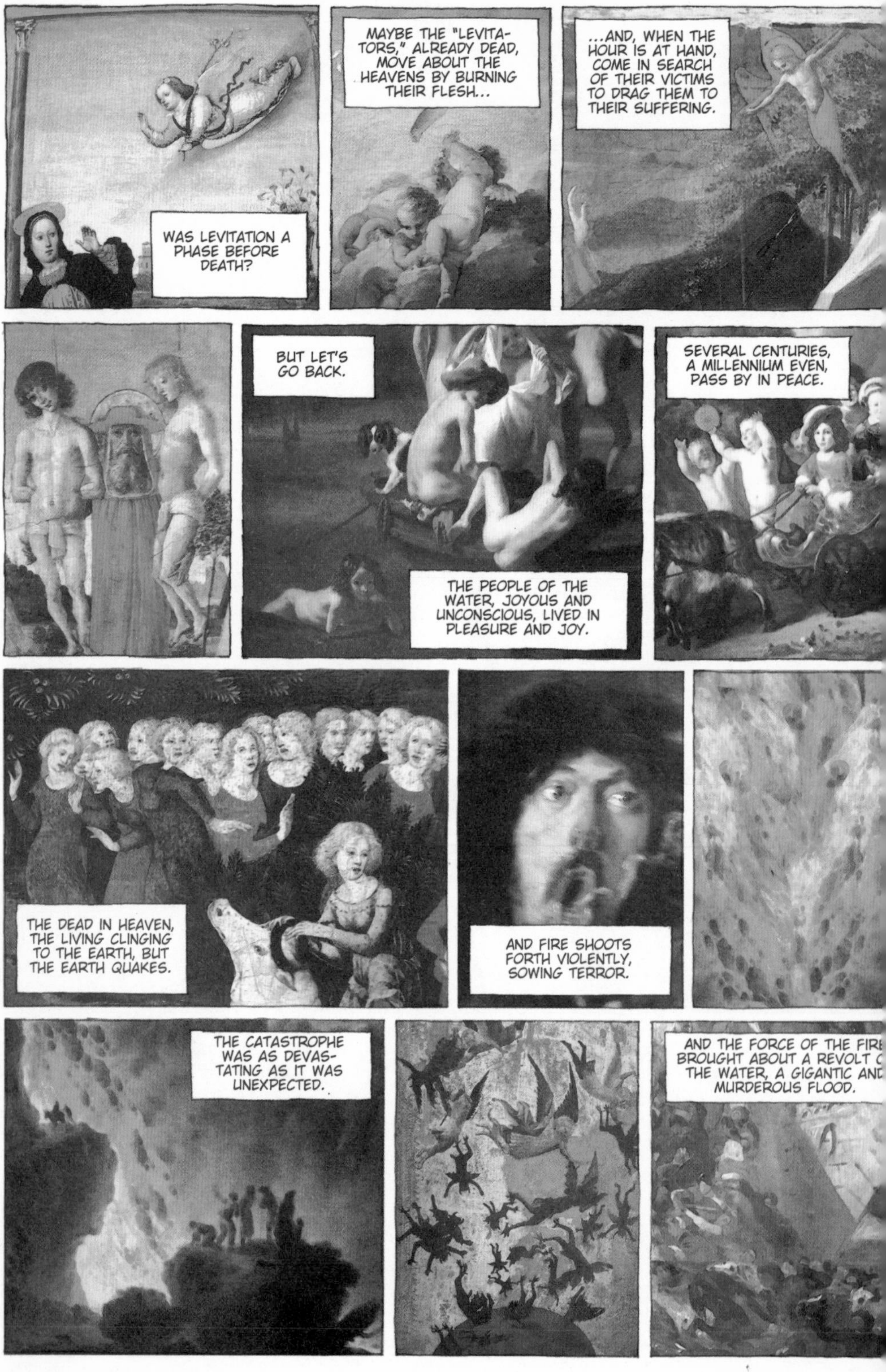
WAS LEVITATION A PHASE BEFORE DEATH?
MAYBE THE "LEVITATORS," ALREADY DEAD, MOVE ABOUT THE HEAVENS BY BURNING THEIR FLESH...
...AND, WHEN THE HOUR IS AT HAND, COME IN SEARCH OF THEIR VICTIMS TO DRAG THEM TO THEIR SUFFERING.
BUT LET'S GO BACK.
THE PEOPLE OF THE WATER, JOYOUS AND UNCONSCIOUS, LIVED IN PLEASURE AND JOY.
SEVERAL CENTURIES, A MILLENNIUM EVEN, PASS BY IN PEACE.
THE DEAD IN HEAVEN, THE LIVING CLINGING TO THE EARTH, BUT THE EARTH QUAKES.
AND FIRE SHOOTS FORTH VIOLENTLY, SOWING TERROR.
THE CATASTROPHE WAS AS DEVASTATING AS IT WAS UNEXPECTED.
AND THE FORCE OF THE FIR
BROUGHT ABOUT A REVOLT
THE WATER, A GIGANTIC AN
MURDEROUS FLOOD.

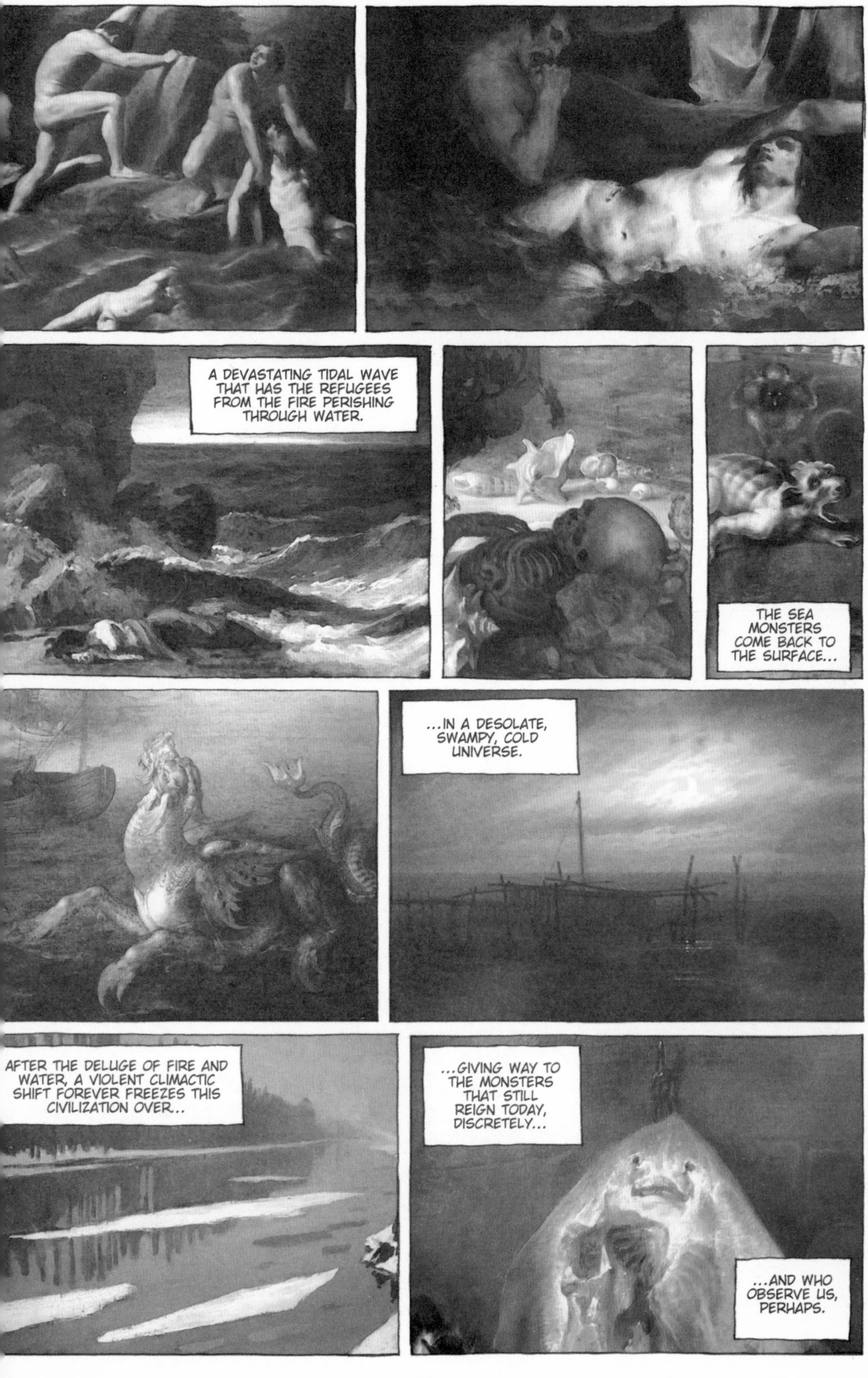
A DEVASTATING TIDAL WAVE THAT HAS THE REFUGEES FROM THE FIRE PERISHING THROUGH WATER.
THE SEA MONSTERS COME BACK TO THE SURFACE...
...IN A DESOLATE, SWAMPY, COLD UNIVERSE.
AFTER THE DELUGE OF FIRE AND WATER, A VIOLENT CLIMACTIC SHIFT FOREVER FREEZES THIS CIVILIZATION OVER...
...GIVING WAY TO THE MONSTERS THAT STILL REIGN TODAY, DISCRETELY...
...AND WHO OBSERVE US, PERHAPS.

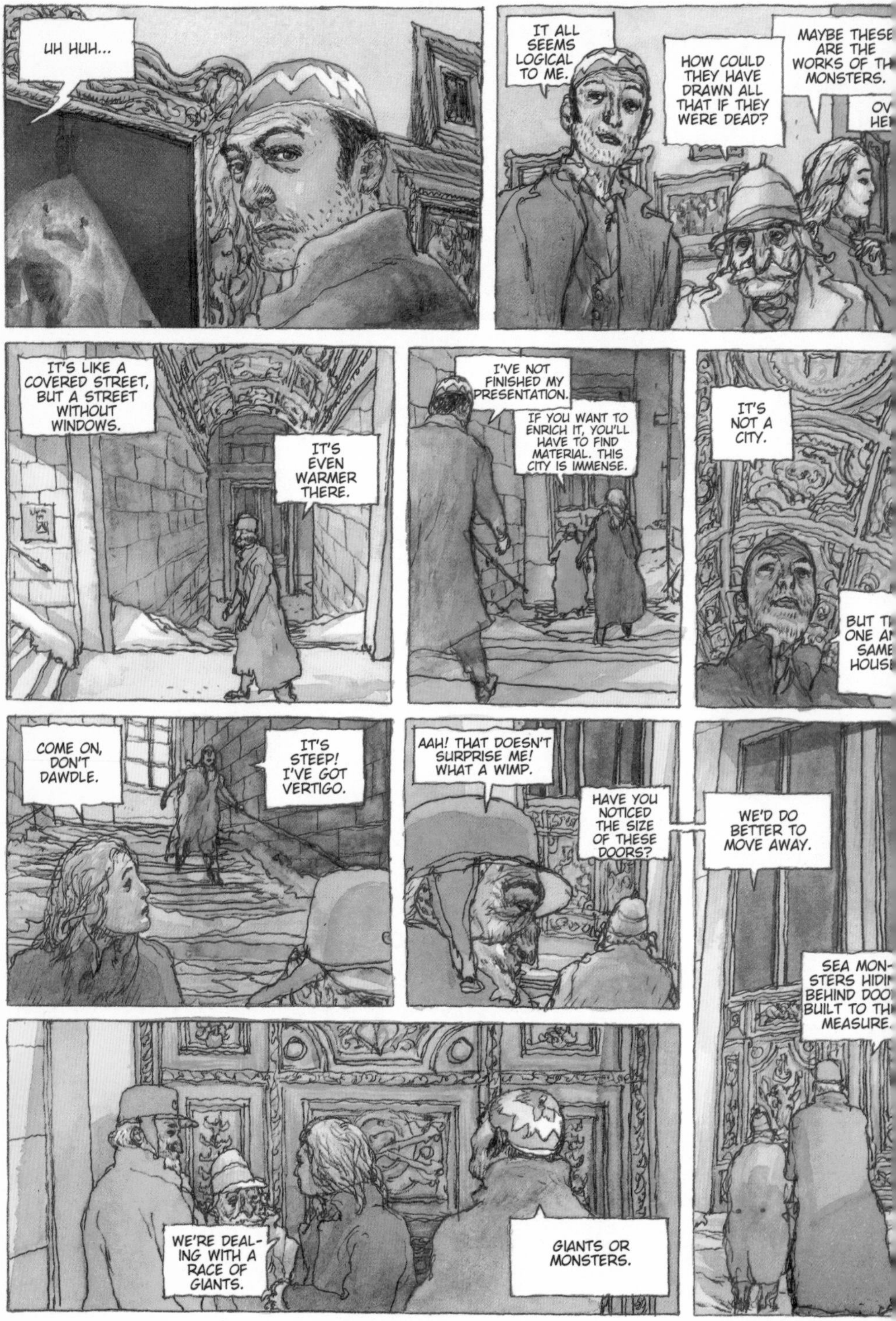

UH HUH...
IT ALL SEEMS LOGICAL TO ME.
HOW COULD THEY HAVE DRAWN ALL THAT IF THEY WERE DEAD?
MAYBE THESE ARE THE WORKS OF TH MONSTERS.
IT'S LIKE A COVERED STREET, BUT A STREET WITHOUT WINDOWS.
IT'S EVEN WARMER THERE.
I'VE NOT FINISHED MY PRESENTATION.
IF YOU WANT TO ENRICH IT, YOU'LL HAVE TO FIND MATERIAL. THIS CITY IS IMMENSE.
IT'S NOT A CITY.
COME ON, DON'T DAWDLE.
IT'S STEEP! I'VE GOT VERTIGO.
AAH! THAT DOESN'T SURPRISE ME! WHAT A WIMP.
HAVE YOU NOTICED THE SIZE OF THESE DOORS?
WE'D DO BETTER TO MOVE AWAY.
WE'RE DEALING WITH A RACE OF GIANTS.
GIANTS OR MONSTERS.

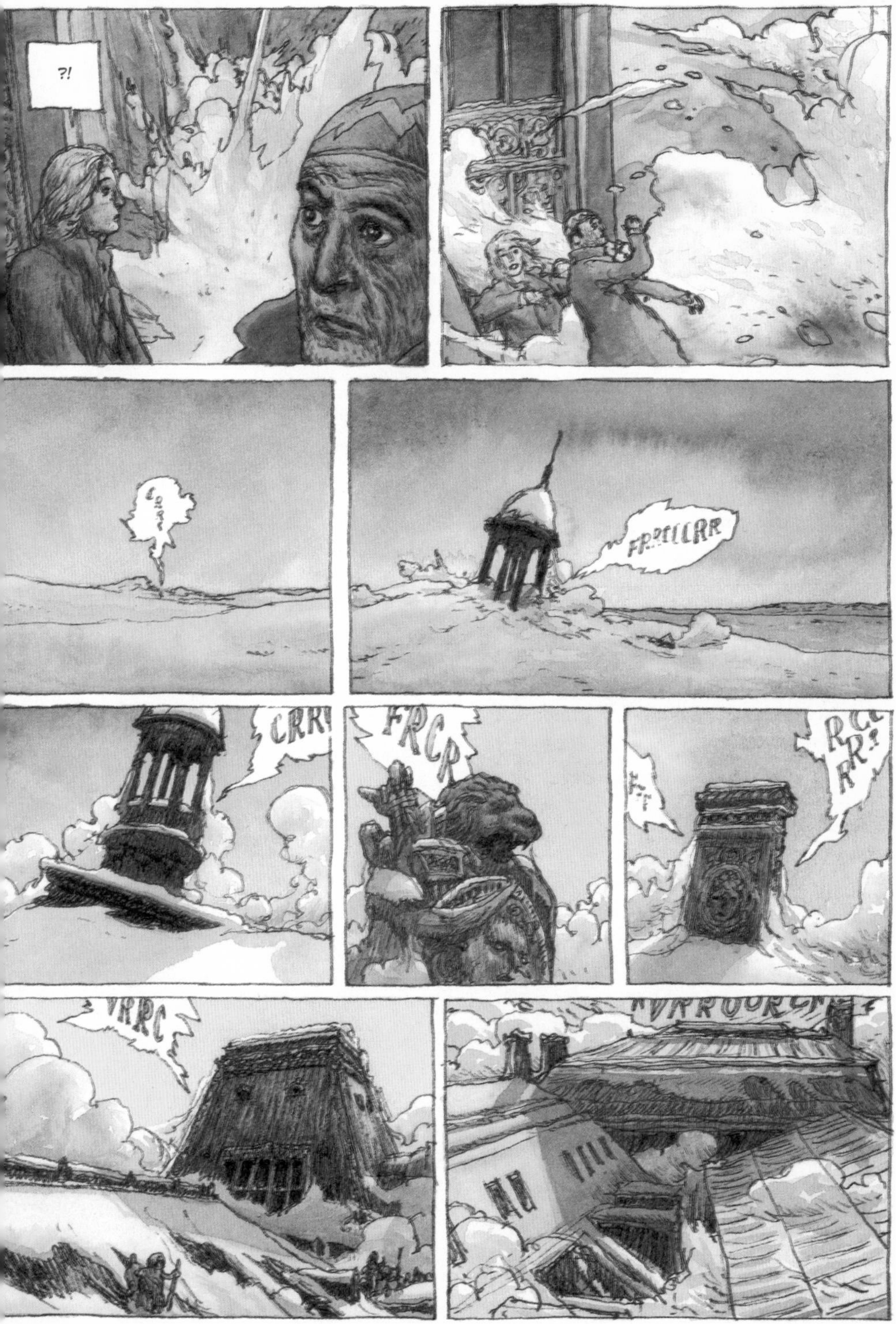
?!
CRR
FRCR
VRRC

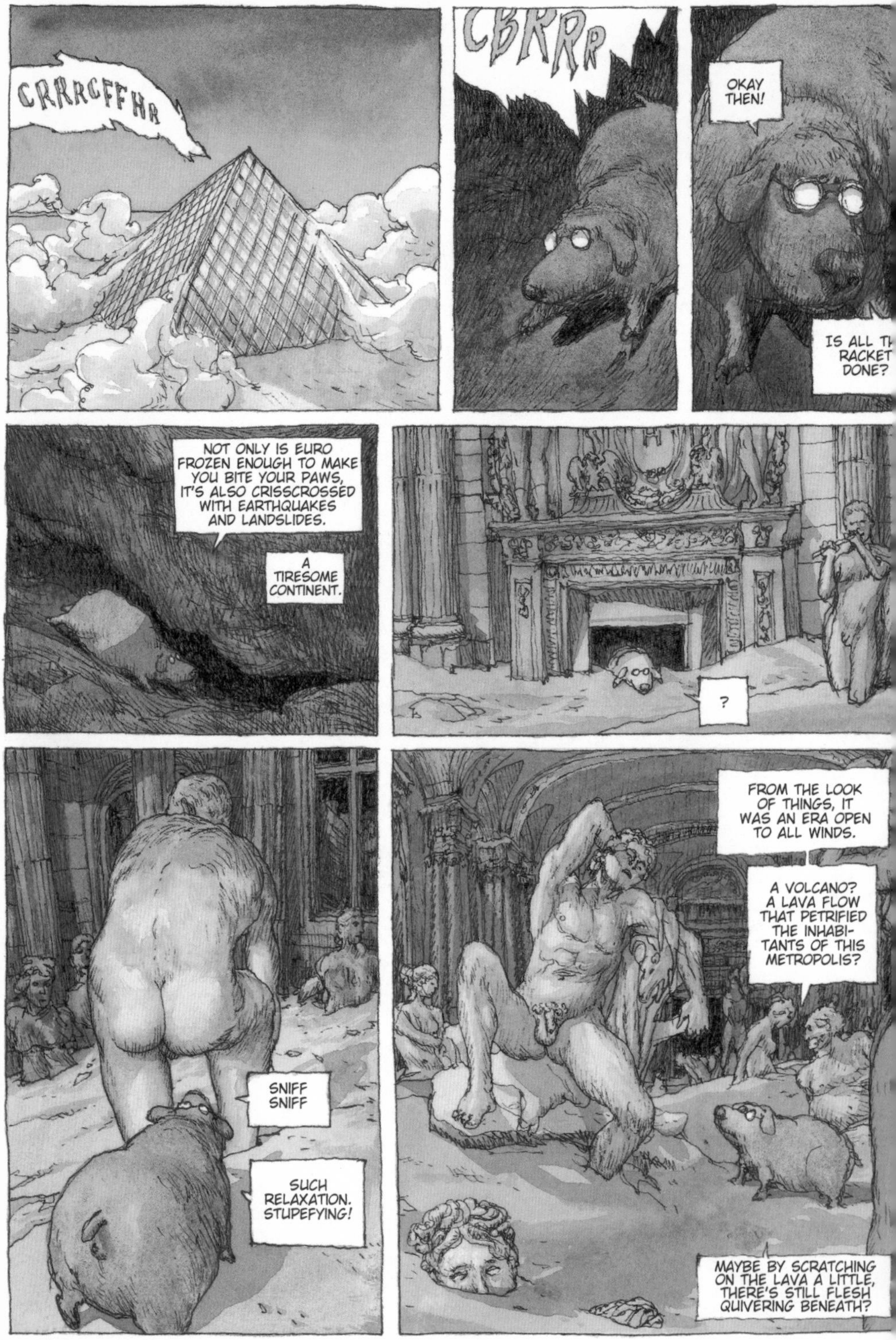

CRRRCFFHR
CBRRR
OKAY THEN!
IS ALL T RACKET DONE?
NOT ONLY IS EURO FROZEN ENOUGH TO MAKE YOU BITE YOUR PAWS, IT'S ALSO CRISSCROSSED WITH EARTHQUAKES AND LANDSLIDES.
A TIRESOME CONTINENT.
?
SNIFF SNIFF
SUCH RELAXATION. STUPEFYING!
FROM THE LOOK OF THINGS, IT WAS AN ERA OPEN TO ALL WINDS.
A VOLCANO? A LAVA FLOW THAT PETRIFIED THE INHABI- TANTS OF THIS METROPOLIS?
MAYBE BY SCRATCHING ON THE LAVA A LITTLE, THERE'S STILL FLESH QUIVERING BENEATH?

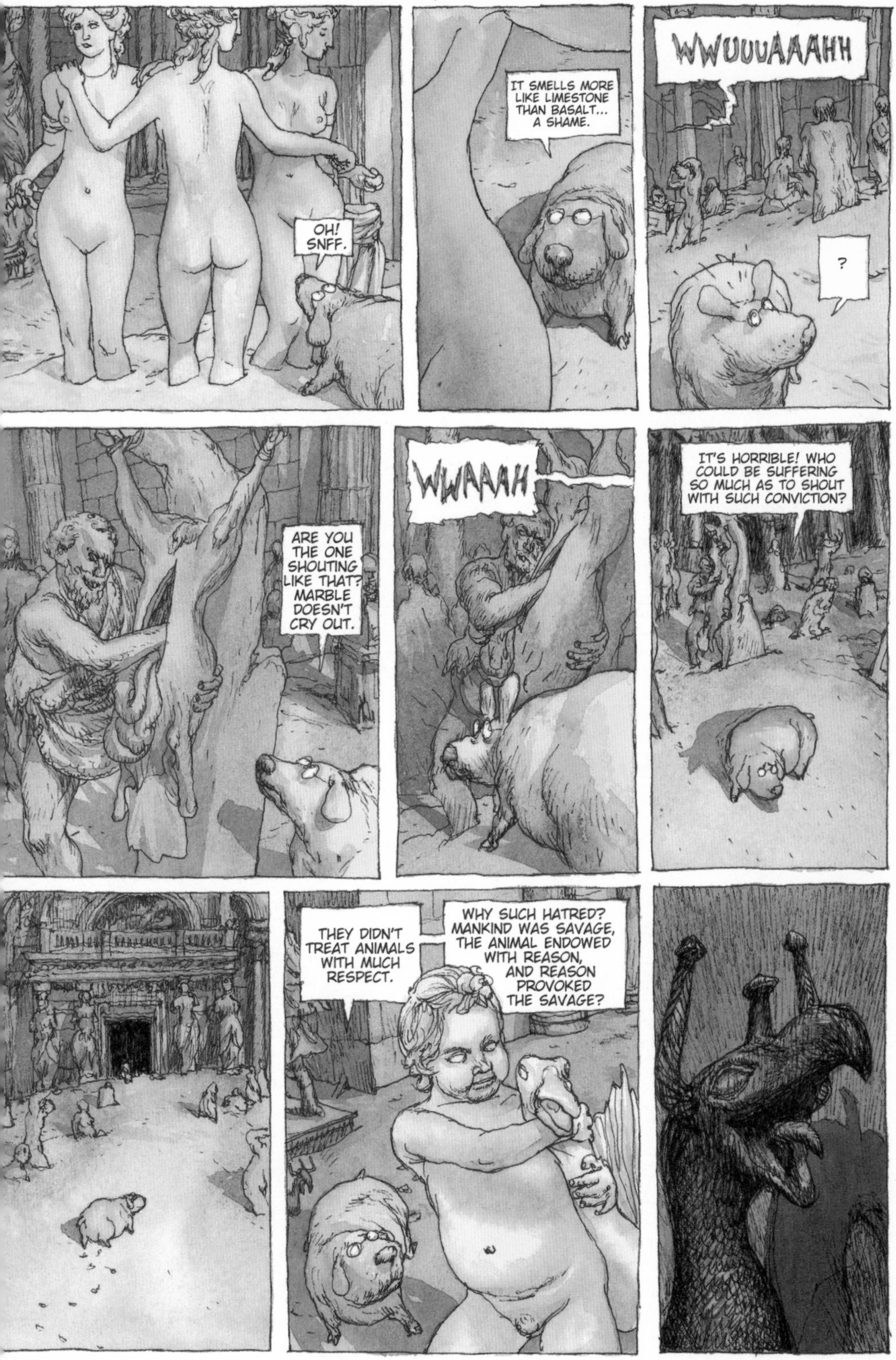
OH! SNFF.
IT SMELLS MORE LIKE LIMESTONE THAN BASALT... A SHAME.
WWUUUAAAHH
?
ARE YOU THE ONE SHOUTING LIKE THAT? MARBLE DOESN'T CRY OUT.
WWAAAH
IT'S HORRIBLE! WHO COULD BE SUFFERING SO MUCH AS TO SHOUT WITH SUCH CONVICTION?
THEY DIDN'T TREAT ANIMALS WITH MUCH RESPECT.
WHY SUCH HATRED? MANKIND WAS SAVAGE, THE ANIMAL ENDOWED WITH REASON, AND REASON PROVOKED THE SAVAGE?

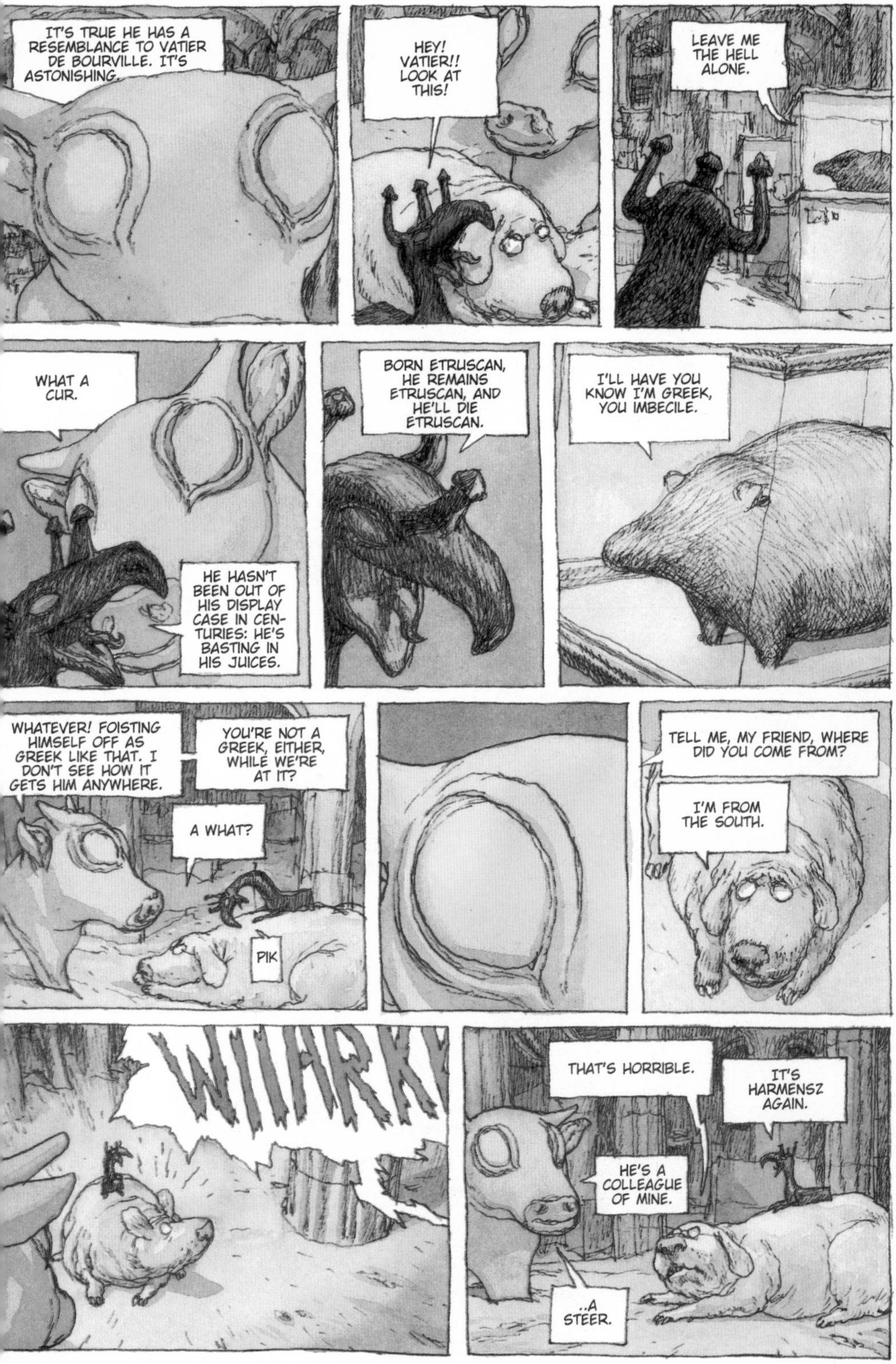
IT'S TRUE HE HAS A RESEMBLANCE TO VATIER DE BOURVILLE. IT'S ASTONISHING.
HEY! VATIER!! LOOK AT THIS!
LEAVE ME THE HELL ALONE.
WHAT A CUR.
HE HASN'T BEEN OUT OF HIS DISPLAY CASE IN CENTURIES: HE'S BASTING IN HIS JUICES.
BORN ETRUSCAN, HE REMAINS ETRUSCAN, AND HE'LL DIE ETRUSCAN.
I'LL HAVE YOU KNOW I'M GREEK, YOU IMBECILE.
WHATEVER! FOISTING HIMSELF OFF AS GREEK LIKE THAT. I DON'T SEE HOW IT GETS HIM ANYWHERE.
YOU'RE NOT A GREEK, EITHER, WHILE WE'RE AT IT?
A WHAT?
PIK
TELL ME, MY FRIEND, WHERE DID YOU COME FROM?
I'M FROM THE SOUTH.
WHARK
THAT'S HORRIBLE.
IT'S HARMENSZ AGAIN.
HE'S A COLLEAGUE OF MINE.
..A STEER.

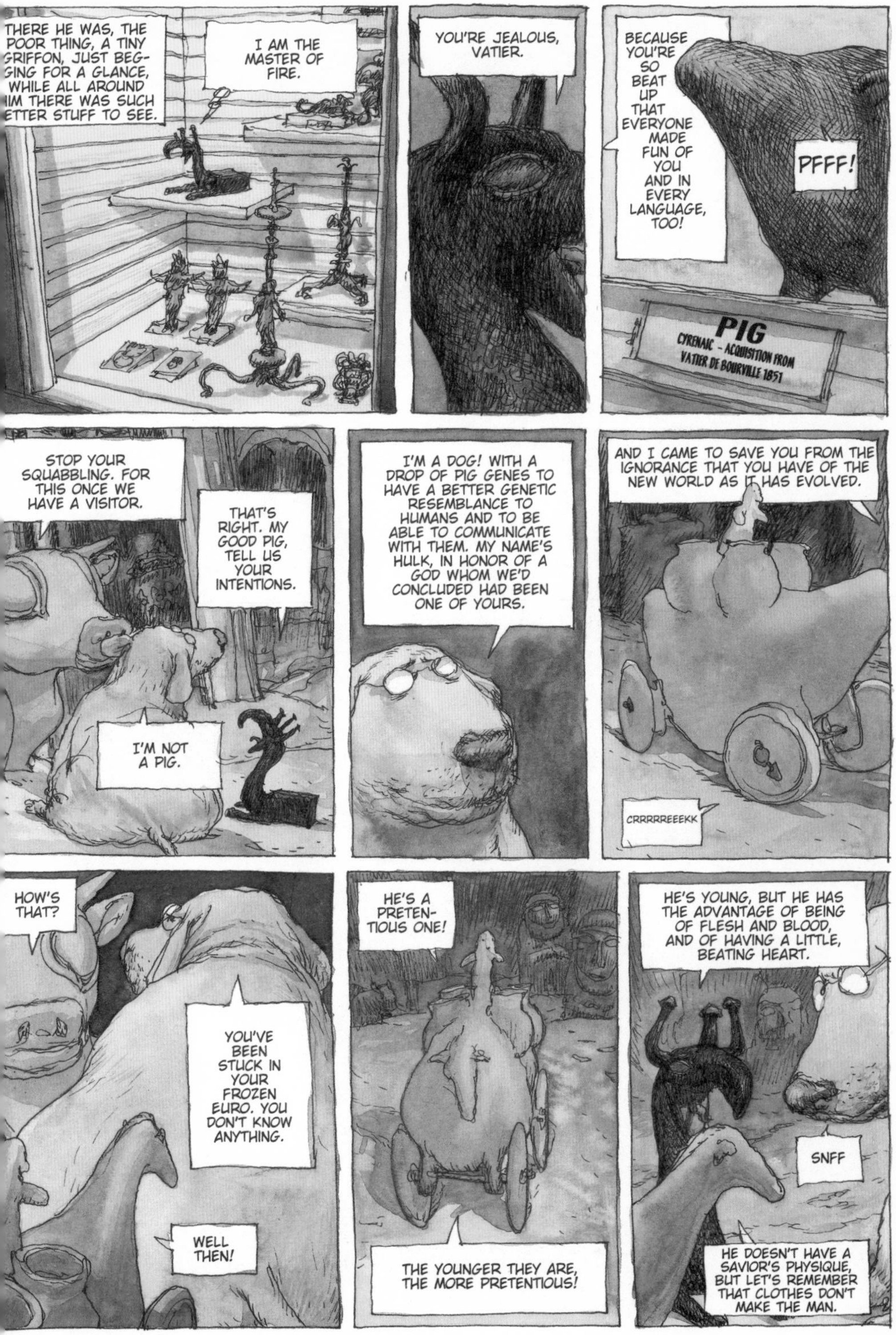

THERE HE WAS, THE POOR THING, A TINY GRIFFON, JUST BEGGING FOR A GLANCE, WHILE ALL AROUND HIM THERE WAS SUCH BETTER STUFF TO SEE.
I AM THE MASTER OF FIRE.
YOU'RE JEALOUS, VATIER.
BECAUSE YOU'RE SO BEAT UP THAT EVERYONE MADE FUN OF YOU AND IN EVERY LANGUAGE, TOO!
PFFF!
PIG
CYRENAIC - ACQUISITION FROM VATIER DE BOURVILLE 1851
STOP YOUR SQUABBLING. FOR THIS ONCE WE HAVE A VISITOR.
THAT'S RIGHT. MY GOOD PIG, TELL US YOUR INTENTIONS.
I'M NOT A PIG.
I'M A DOG! WITH A DROP OF PIG GENES TO HAVE A BETTER GENETIC RESEMBLANCE TO HUMANS AND TO BE ABLE TO COMMUNICATE WITH THEM. MY NAME'S HULK, IN HONOR OF A GOD WHOM WE'D CONCLUDED HAD BEEN ONE OF YOURS.
AND I CAME TO SAVE YOU FROM THE IGNORANCE THAT YOU HAVE OF THE NEW WORLD AS IT HAS EVOLVED.
CRRRRREEEKK
HOW'S THAT?
YOU'VE BEEN STUCK IN YOUR FROZEN EURO. YOU DON'T KNOW ANYTHING.
WELL THEN!
HE'S A PRETENTIOUS ONE!
THE YOUNGER THEY ARE, THE MORE PRETENTIOUS!
HE'S YOUNG, BUT HE HAS THE ADVANTAGE OF BEING OF FLESH AND BLOOD, AND OF HAVING A LITTLE, BEATING HEART.
SNFF
HE DOESN'T HAVE A SAVIOR'S PHYSIQUE, BUT LET'S REMEMBER THAT CLOTHES DON'T MAKE THE MAN.

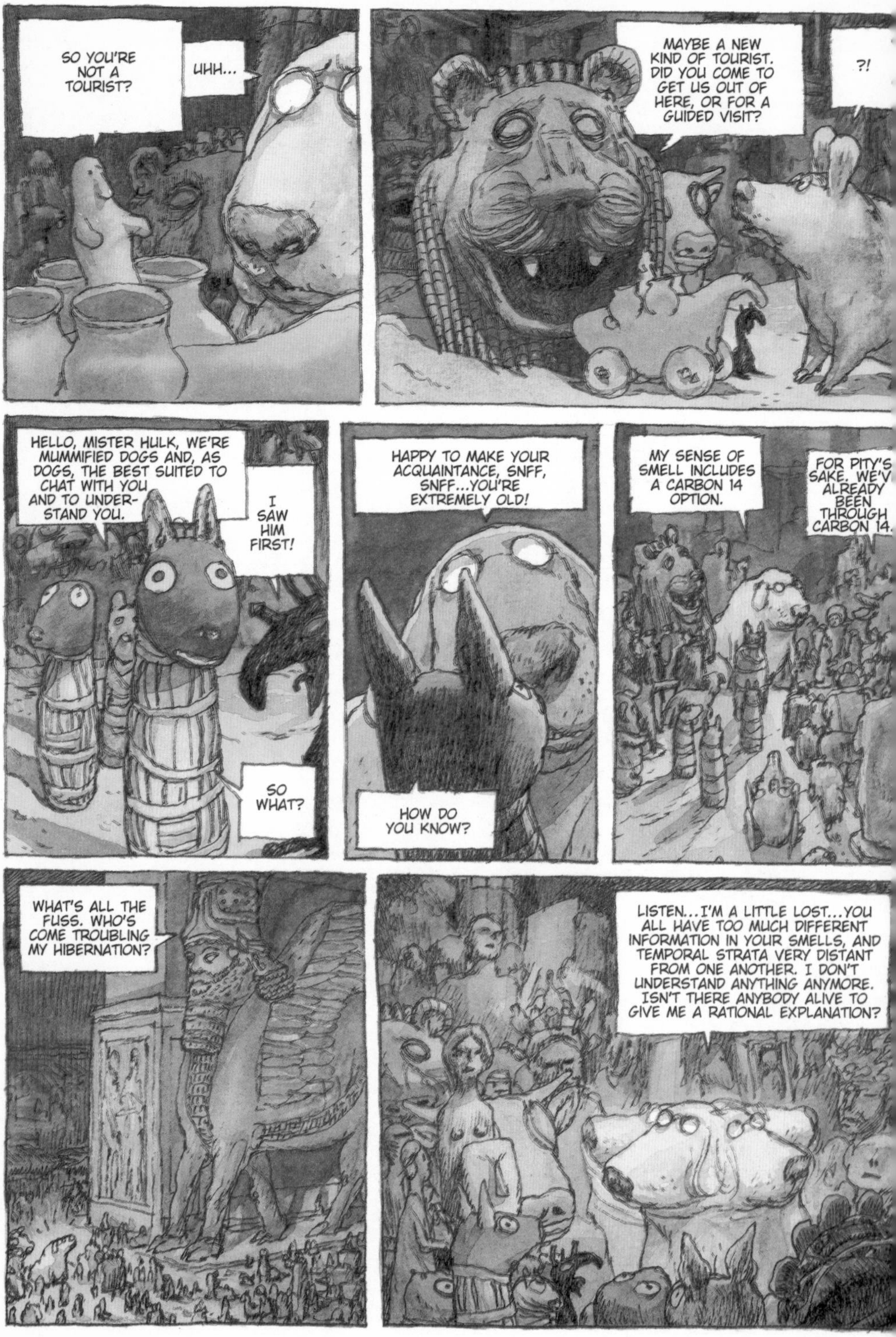
SO YOU'RE NOT A TOURIST?
UHH...
MAYBE A NEW KIND OF TOURIST. DID YOU COME TO GET US OUT OF HERE, OR FOR A GUIDED VISIT?
?!
HELLO, MISTER HULK, WE'RE MUMMIFIED DOGS AND, AS DOGS, THE BEST SUITED TO CHAT WITH YOU AND TO UNDERSTAND YOU.
I SAW HIM FIRST!
SO WHAT?
HAPPY TO MAKE YOUR ACQUAINTANCE, SNFF, SNFF...YOU'RE EXTREMELY OLD!
HOW DO YOU KNOW?
MY SENSE OF SMELL INCLUDES A CARBON 14 OPTION.
FOR PITY'S SAKE, WE'V ALREADY BEEN THROUGH CARBON 14.
WHAT'S ALL THE FUSS. WHO'S COME TROUBLING MY HIBERNATION?
LISTEN...I'M A LITTLE LOST...YOU ALL HAVE TOO MUCH DIFFERENT INFORMATION IN YOUR SMELLS, AND TEMPORAL STRATA VERY DISTANT FROM ONE ANOTHER. I DON'T UNDERSTAND ANYTHING ANYMORE. ISN'T THERE ANYBODY ALIVE TO GIVE ME A RATIONAL EXPLANATION?

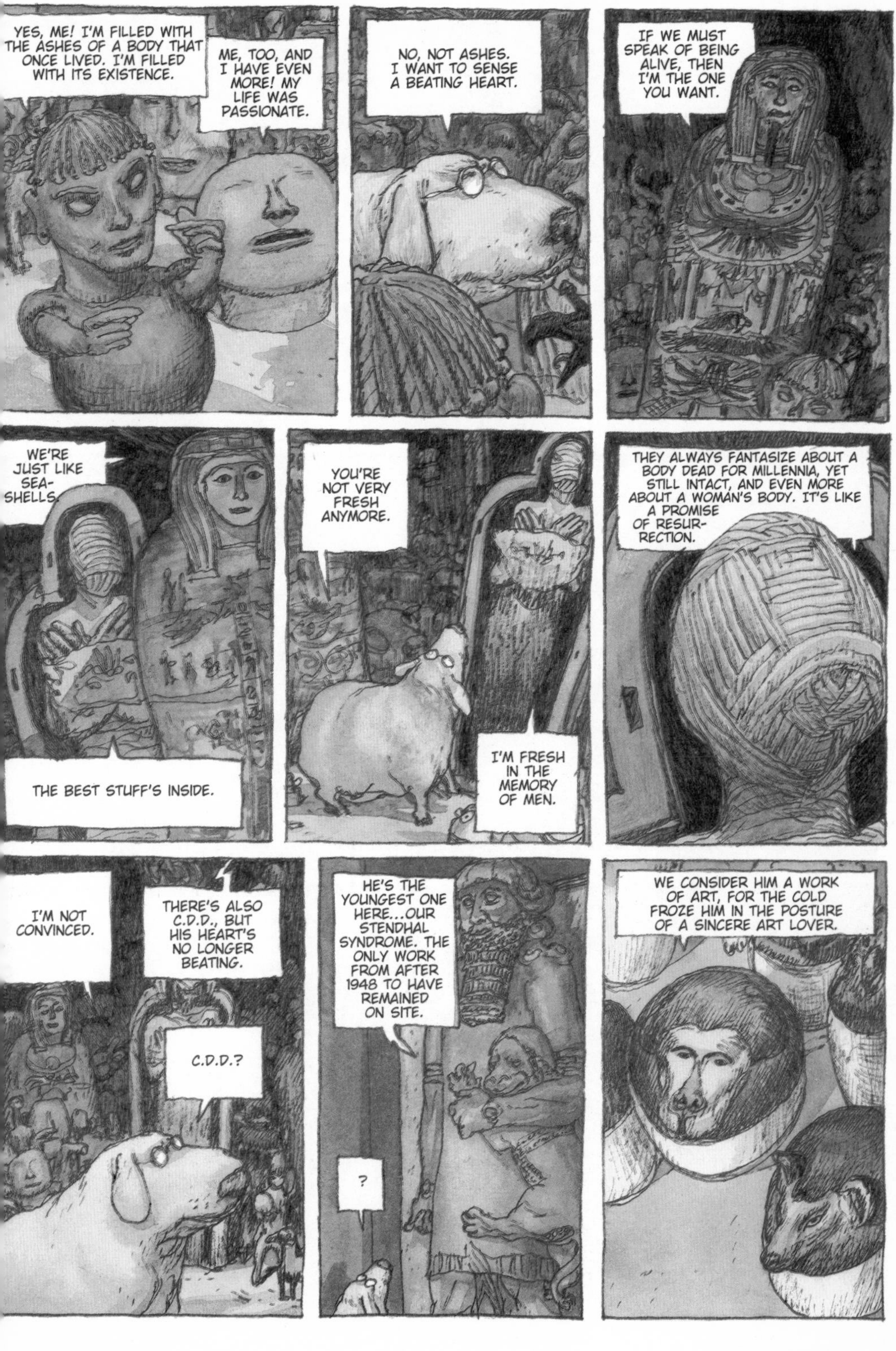

YES, ME! I'M FILLED WITH THE ASHES OF A BODY THAT ONCE LIVED. I'M FILLED WITH ITS EXISTENCE.
ME, TOO, AND I HAVE EVEN MORE! MY LIFE WAS PASSIONATE.
NO, NOT ASHES. I WANT TO SENSE A BEATING HEART.
IF WE MUST SPEAK OF BEING ALIVE, THEN I'M THE ONE YOU WANT.
WE'RE JUST LIKE SEA-SHELLS.
THE BEST STUFF'S INSIDE.
YOU'RE NOT VERY FRESH ANYMORE.
I'M FRESH IN THE MEMORY OF MEN.
THEY ALWAYS FANTASIZE ABOUT A BODY DEAD FOR MILLENNIA, YET STILL INTACT, AND EVEN MORE ABOUT A WOMAN'S BODY. IT'S LIKE A PROMISE OF RESUR-RECTION.
I'M NOT CONVINCED.
THERE'S ALSO C.D.D., BUT HIS HEART'S NO LONGER BEATING.
C.D.D.?
HE'S THE YOUNGEST ONE HERE...OUR STENDHAL SYNDROME. THE ONLY WORK FROM AFTER 1948 TO HAVE REMAINED ON SITE.
?
WE CONSIDER HIM A WORK OF ART, FOR THE COLD FROZE HIM IN THE POSTURE OF A SINCERE ART LOVER.

PREMATURELY REMOVED FROM OUR PALACE TO WANDER ABOUT THE COUNTRYSIDE, WE ENDED UP AT THE CASTLE OF CHAMBORD BECAUSE IT WAS REMOTE FROM THE BOMBARDMENTS.

BEFORE DEPARTING AGAIN FOR SOUCHES WHILE AWAITING OUR COLLEAGUES, THE WINGED VICTORY OF SAMOTHRACE HAD TROUBLE GETTING ABOUT WITH HER THREE TONS.

OTHER WORKS ARRIVED VIA SECRET CONVOYS IN THE STREAMS OF REFUGEES. WE THEN LEFT FOR LOC-DIEU, ON A SPLENDID SUMMER DAY, WHEN WE HAD A NAP ON THE HAY, AFTER SEVERAL MONTHS OF HUMIDITY.

COMFORT WAS LIMITED, AND LIFE ENCLOSED IN WOODEN BOXES SEEMED BORING TO ME. MY HORSE IS SPIRITED. LUCKILY, A SMALL HOLE ALLOWED ME TO TAKE ADVANTAGE OF THE LIGHT.

BUT OUR ENEMIES WERE APPROACHING. HITLER FERVENTLY DESIRED TO SEE US IN HIS LINZ MUSEUM. A NEW DEPARTURE, THEN, FOR MONTAUBAN...

...TO THE INGRES MUSEUM. FINALLY, A LOCATION WORTHY OF OUR STATURE. AN INOPPORTUNE FLOOD OBLIGED US TO FLEE ONCE AGAIN.

THEN A CHASE GOT UNDERWAY WITH ARMORED CARS. "TITIAN WAS A PAINTER," WHICH SEEMS OBVIOUS, WAS THE CODED PHRASE FOR DEPARTURE: WE TRUDGED ALONG THE VALLEYS OF QUERCY.

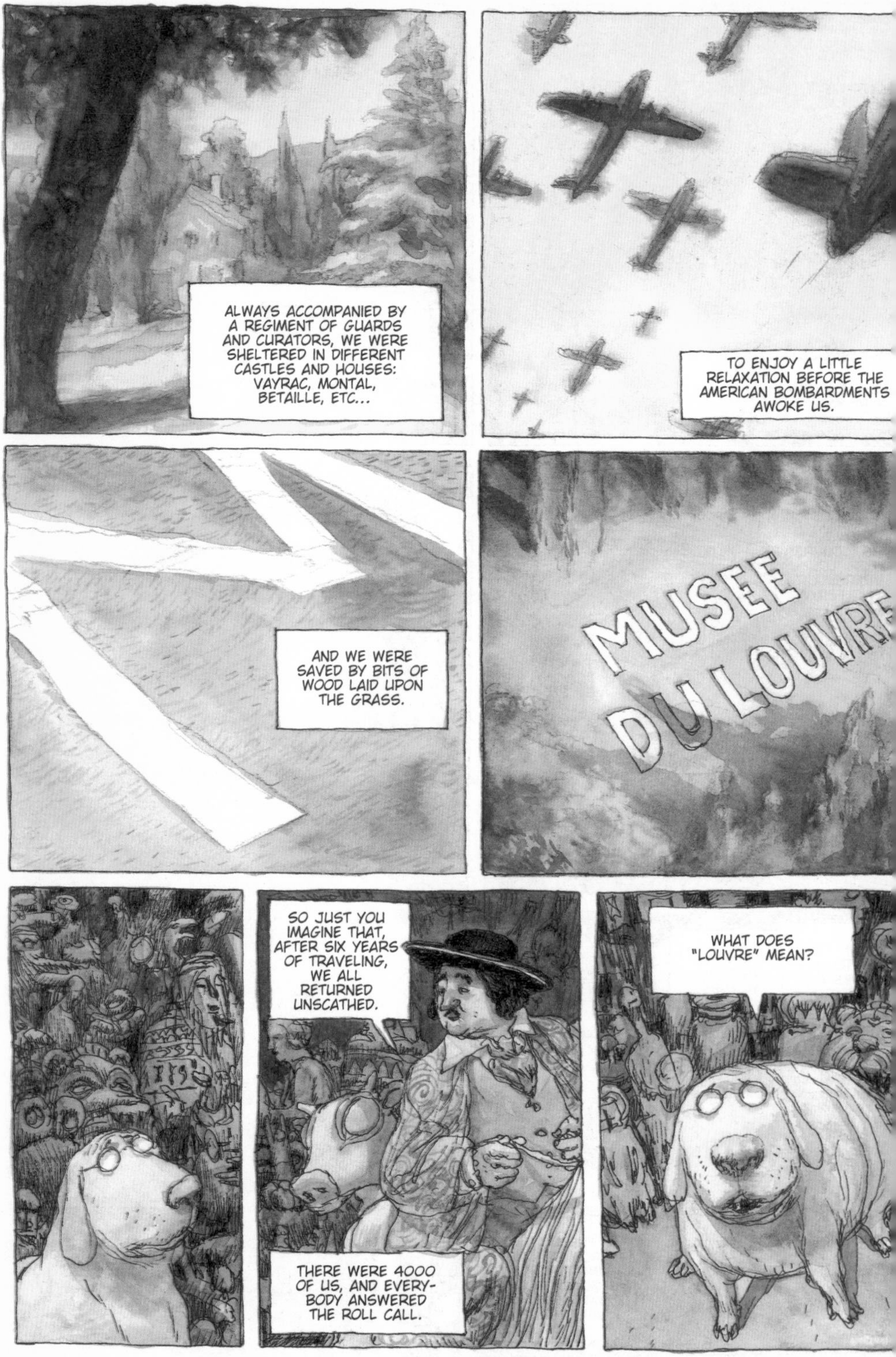
ALWAYS ACCOMPANIED BY A REGIMENT OF GUARDS AND CURATORS, WE WERE SHELTERED IN DIFFERENT CASTLES AND HOUSES: VAYRAC, MONTAL, BETAILLE, ETC...
TO ENJOY A LITTLE RELAXATION BEFORE THE AMERICAN BOMBARDMENTS AWOKE US.
AND WE WERE SAVED BY BITS OF WOOD LAID UPON THE GRASS.
MUSEE DU LOUVRE
SO JUST YOU IMAGINE THAT, AFTER SIX YEARS OF TRAVELING, WE ALL RETURNED UNSCATHED.
THERE WERE 4000 OF US, AND EVERY-BODY ANSWERED THE ROLL CALL.
WHAT DOES "LOUVRE" MEAN?

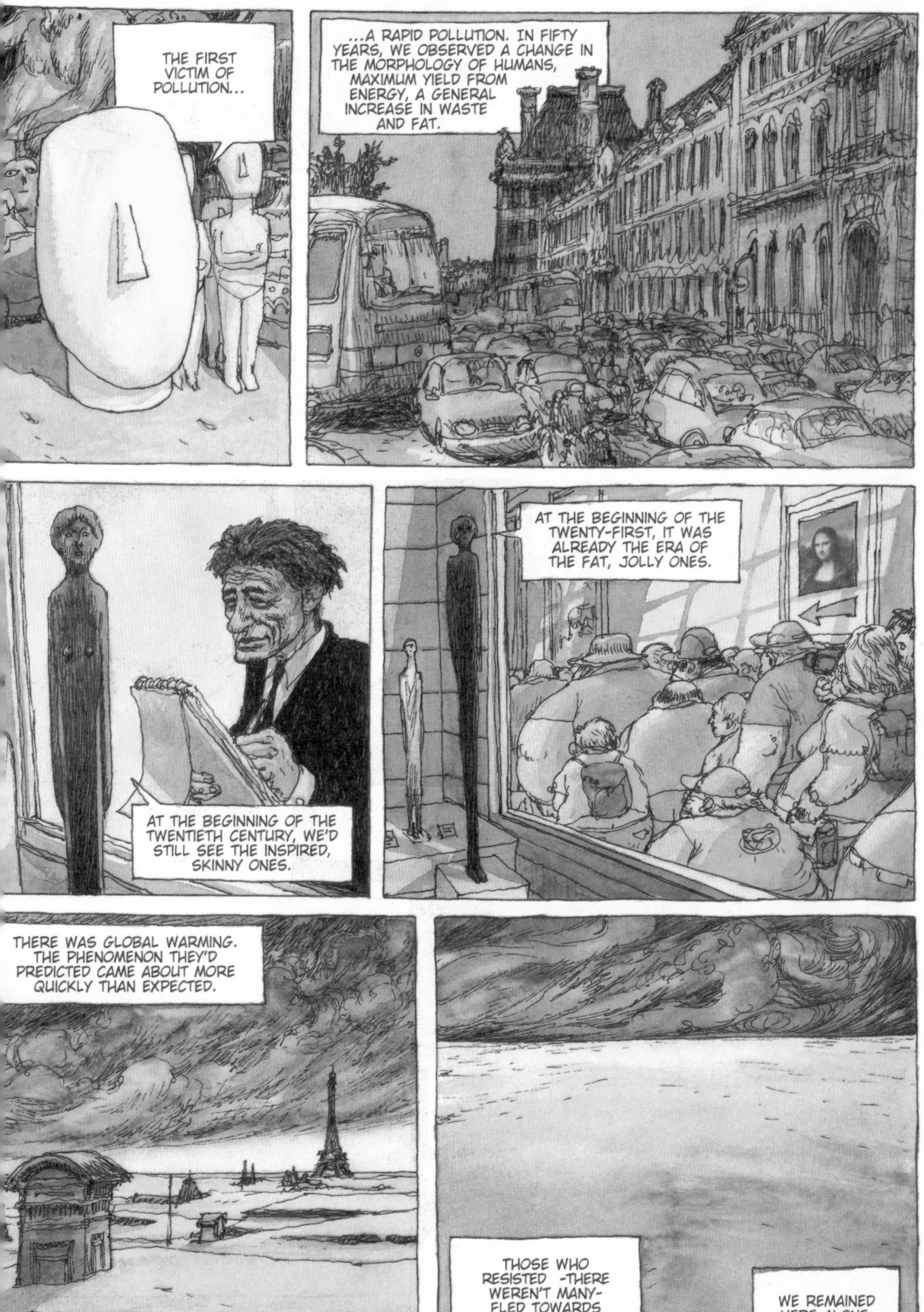
THE FIRST VICTIM OF POLLUTION...
...A RAPID POLLUTION. IN FIFTY YEARS, WE OBSERVED A CHANGE IN THE MORPHOLOGY OF HUMANS, MAXIMUM YIELD FROM ENERGY, A GENERAL INCREASE IN WASTE AND FAT.
AT THE BEGINNING OF THE TWENTIETH CENTURY, WE'D STILL SEE THE INSPIRED, SKINNY ONES.
AT THE BEGINNING OF THE TWENTY-FIRST, IT WAS ALREADY THE ERA OF THE FAT, JOLLY ONES.
THERE WAS GLOBAL WARMING. THE PHENOMENON THEY'D PREDICTED CAME ABOUT MORE QUICKLY THAN EXPECTED.
THOSE WHO RESISTED -THERE WEREN'T MANY- FLED TOWARDS THE SOUTH.
WE REMAINED HERE ALONE.

73

74

List of works chosen by the
author in order of appearance

François André Vincent
Zeuxis and the girls of Crotone, 1789
Oil on canvas, 325 cm x 415 cm
Louis XVI Collection, Inv 8453
Sully Pavilion, Third Floor, Room 53

PAGE 45
François Boucher
The Odalisk, 1745
Oil on canvas, 53.5 cm x 64.5 cm
Bequest of Baron Basile de Schlinchting, 1914, RF 2140
Sully Pavilion, Third Floor, Room 40

Jean-Auguste Dominique Ingres
Angelique (detail), circa 1819
Canvas, 85 cm x 143 cm
Bequest of Paul Cosson, 1926, RF 2520
Sully Pavilion, Third Floor, Room 60

Jean-Siméon Chardin
The Monkey Painter, 1739-1740
Oil on canvas, 73 cm x 59 cm
Bequest of Dr. Louis La Caze, 1869, MI 1033
Sully Pavilion, Third Floor, Room 39

Domenico Mecarino, known as **Beccafumi**
Saint Anthony and the miracle of the mule
Oil on canvas, 33 cm x 51 cm
Acquired in 1966, RF 1966-2
Denon Pavilion, Second Floor, Room 8

Jacob Jordaens
Diana resting, circa 1640-1650
Oil on canvas, 203 cm x 264 cm
Gift of the Society of Friends of the Museum, 1982, RF 1982-11
Richelieu Pavilion, Third Floor, Room 26

Antonio Allegri, known as **Corregio**
Venus and Eros discovered by a satyr, once known
as *Jupiter and Antiope,* circa 1524-1525
Oil on canvas, 188 cm x 125 cm
Acquired by Louis XIV from the heirs of Mazarin, 1665, Inv 42
Denon Pavilion, Second Floor, Room 8

Petrus-Paulus Rubens
The Virgin and Child, surrounded by the Innocents,
once titled *Virgin with Children*
Oil on canvas, 138 cm x 100 cm
Collection of Louis XIV, acquired in 1671, Inv 1763
Richelieu Pavilion, Third Floor, Room 21

Nicolas Poussin
The Spring, (reversed detail), circa 1660-1664
Oil on canvas, 118 cm x 160 cm
Collection of Louis XIV, acquired by the Duke of
Richelieu in 1665, Inv 7303
Richelieu Pavilion, Third Floor, Room 16

Stefano di Giovanni di Console, known as **Sassetta**
*The Fortunate Ranieri Rasini delivers the poor from a prison in
Florence,* between 1437 and 1444
Oil on canvas, 43 cm x 63 cm
Gift of the Society for Friends of the Louvre, 1965, RF 1965-2
Denon Pavilion, Second Floor, Room 4

Sano di Pietro
*The death of the saint and his appearance
to Saint Cyril of Jerusalem*
Belongs to *Scenes of the life of Saint Jerome,* 1444
Oil on wood, 23 cm x 35 cm, MI 473
Denon Pavilion, Second Floor, Room of the Sept-Mètres

PAGE 46
Carlo Braccesco
The Annunciation, central panel of a triptych, circa 1480-1500

Oil on wood, 158 cm x 107 cm
Acquired in 1812, Inv 1410
Denon Pavilion, Second Floor, Room 5

François Boucher
The Kidnapping of Europa (detail), 1747
Canvas, 160 cm x 193 cm
Collection of Louis XV, acquired in 1747, Inv 2714
Sully Pavilion, Third Floor, Room 46

Francesco di Stefano, known as **Pesellino**
The Stigmatization of Saint Francis, circa 1440-1445
Oil on wood, 32 cm x 94 cm.
Received in the Louvre in 1814, Inv 418
Denon Pavilion, Second Floor, Room 4

Pietro di Cristoforo Vannucci, known as **Perugino**
Saint Jerome saves two hanged men
(right panel of a triptych), circa 1473-1475
Oil on wood, 30 cm x 28 cm
Ancient Campana Collection, Rome, Louvre 1863, MI 481
Denon Pavilion, Second Floor, Room 4

Nicolaes Maes
The Bathing
Oil on cavas, 72 cm x 91 cm
Bequest of Baron Basile de Schlichting, 1914, RF 2132
Richelieu Pavilion, Third Floor, Room 32

Ferdinand Bol
The Noble children (of the Trip family?) in goat-drawn cart, 1654
Oil on canvas, 211 cm x 249 cm.
Séquestre Miliotty, 1799, Inv 1062
Richelieu Pavilion, Third Floor, Room 33

Liberale da Verona
The Kidnapping of Europa, circa 1470
Painted panel, 39 cm x 118 cm
Former Campana collection, received in the Louvre in 1863, MI 585
Denon Pavilion, Second Floor, Room 4

Joos van Craesbeek
The Smoker
Oil on canvas, 41 cm x 32 cm
Bequest of Dr. Louis La Caze, 1869, MI 906
Richelieu Pavilion, Third Floor, Room 23

Michael Wutky
Eruption of Vesuvius, circa 1780
Oil on canvas, 78 cm x 64 cm
Acquired in 1998 due to the sponsorship of
the Saint Gobain Company, RF 1998-37
Richelieu Pavilion, Third Floor, Room F

Maître des anges rebelles (Master of the Rebellious Angels)
The Fall of the rebellious angels, circa 1340-1345
Distemper on wood set on canvas, 64 cm x 29 cm
On loan from the Bourges Museum, 1967, D.L. 1967-1-b
Denon Pavilion, Second Floor, Room 4

PAGE 47
Antonio Carracci
The Deluge, circa 1616-1618
Canvas, 166 cm x 247 cm
Collection of Louis XIV (gift of the heirs of Cardinal Mazarin in 1661), Inv 230
Denon Pavilion, Second Floor, Room 12

Eugène Delacroix
Dante and Virgil in the Inferno, also known as
Dante's Boat (detail), salon of 1822
Oil on canvas, 189 cm x 241 cm
Acquired at the Salon of 1822, Inv 3820
Denon Pavilion, Second Floor, Room 77

Théodore Géricault
The Tempest, or *the Flotsam*
Oil on canvas, 19 cm x 25 cm, RF 784
Sully Pavilion, Third Floor, Room 61

Joachim Wtewael
Perseus rescuing Andromeda (detail), 1611
Oil on canvas, 180 cm x 150 cm
Gift of the Society of Friends of the Musée du Louvre, 1982, P, RF 1982-51
Richelieu Pavilion, Third Floor, Room 13

Raffaelo Santi, known as Raphael
Saint Michael (detail), circa 1504
Oil on wood, 30.9 cm x 26.5 cm
Collection of Louis XIV (acquired in 1661), Inv 608
Denon Pavilion, Second Floor, Room 5

Caspar David Friedrich
Seacoast by moonlight, 1818
Oil on canvas, 22 x 30 cm
Gift of the Society of Friends of the Louvre, RF 2000-3
Richelieu Pavilion, Third Floor, Room E

Claude Monet
Ice on the Seine at Bougival
Oil on canvas, 65 cm x 81 cm
Hélène and Victor Lyon Donation, 1961, RF 1961-62
Sully Pavilion, Third Floor, Room C

Jean-Siméon Chardin
The Stingray, before 1728
Oil on canvas, 114 cm x 146 cm
Collection of the Académie, Inv. 3197
Sully Pavilion, Second Floor, Room 38

PAGE 50
Hermes putting on a sandal, Roman work, 2nd century A.D.
Discovered in the Theatre of Marcellus in Rome. Marble of Pentelichus for the body, 161 cm. Received in the Louvre in 1797, MR 238/Ma 83
Sully Pavilion, Ground floor, Room 17.

Edmé Bouchardon
Sleeping faun, 1726-30
Marble, 184 cm x 142 cm x 119 cm
Received in the Louvre in 1892
Richelieu Pavilion, Mezzanine, Puget Court

PAGE 51
The Three Graces, Roman work of the Imperial era, 2nd century, A.D.(?)
Rome, Mount Cellius, Villa Cornovaglia
Marble, 119 cm x 85 cm
Former Borghese Collection in Rome, purchased in 1807, MR 211/Ma 287
Sully Pavilion, Ground floor, Room 17

Old man skinning an animal, known as *"The Rustic Skinner,"*
Roman work of the Imperial era, 1st or 2nd century A.D.
Marble, 107 cm
Former Albani Collection, seized by Napoleon, re-purchased
by Louis XVIII in 1815, Ma 517
Sully Pavilion, Ground floor, Room 17

Child and goose, Roman work of the Imperial era, 1st or 2nd century,
A.D., Discovered in 1792 in the Villa Quintili in Rome
Marble, 92.7 cm
Former Braschi Collection in Rome, seized by Napoleon by virtue of the
Treaty of Tolentino in 1797, Received in the Louvre in 1799, Ma 40
Sully Pavilion, Ground floor, Room 17

PAGE 52
Rhyton with a bull's head, Late Minoan, 1400-1200, B.C.
Terracotta, 16.4 cm x 16 cm
Clermont-Ganneau Mission, 1896, CA 909
Denon Pavilion, Mezzanine, Room 1

PAGE 53
Pig, from Cyrenaica

5.1 cm x 9.6 cm
Vattier de Bourville Acquisition, 1851
Sully Pavilion, Second Floor, Room 36

PAGE 55
Animal shown loaded with amphorae, 700-650 B.C.
19 cm x 25 cm
Acquisition 1910, CA 1841
Sully Pavilion, Second Floor, Room 36

PAGE 56
Head of Lion-Temple guard,
beginning of the second millennium B.C., Babylon
Terracotta
Acquired in 1947, AO 19807
Richelieu Pavilion, Ground floor, Room 3

Cat mummies
52.5 cm x 13 cm, N 2889, E 2811, N 2812, N 3505
Sully Pavilion, Ground floor, Room 19

Androcephalous winged bulls, 721-705 B.C.
Khorsabad, Palace of Sargon II of Assyria
Gypsum, 420 cm x 436 cm
P. E. Botta Excavation, 1843-44, AO 19857
Richelieu Pavilion, Ground floor, Room 4

PAGE 57
Canopic jar, Second half of the 6th century, B.C., Chiusi, Italy.
Terracotta, 50 cm
Purchased 1851, D 162
Denon Pavilion, Ground floor, Room 19

Lid of masculine canopic jar
First half of the 6th century, B.C., D 163
Denon Pavilion, Ground floor, Room 19

Assyrian hero mastering a lion
Khorsabad, Palace of Sargon II of Assyria
450 cm x 188 cm x 22 cm
P. E. Botta Excavation 1843-44, AO 19861
Richelieu Pavilion, Ground floor, Room 4

Four canopic jars of Horemsaf
Late Period, 664-332 B.C.
Egyptian alabaster, 36.5 cm
E 18876, E 18877, E 18879
Sully Pavilion, Ground floor, Room 15

PAGE 58
Oenochoe in the form of a woman's head, circa 310-290 B.C.
61.5 cm x 21.7 cm
Campana Collection, 1861, B 489
Sully Pavilion, Second Floor, Room 37

Aphrodite standing on a goose, circa 500-475 B.C.
Boetia, 222 cm x 18.5 cm
Picard Gift, 1908, CA 1747
Sully Pavilion, Second Floor, Room 36

Warrior from the vicinity of Viterbo, beginning of the 5th century B.C.
BR 4225
Denon Pavilion, Ground floor, Room 18

PAGE 60
Vincenzo Catena
Giangiorgio Trissino, circa 1525-27
Oil on canvas, 72 cm x 63 cm, RF 2098
Denon Pavilion, Second Floor, Grand Gallery, Room 5

Juste de Gand and Pedro Berruguete
Saint Jerome-Studiolo d'Urbino, circa 1476
Oil on wood, 116 cm x 68 cm
MI 649
Richelieu Pavilion, Third Floor, Room 6

OTHER
LATITUDES

AKRON SERIES IN POETRY

Akron Series in Poetry

Mary Biddinger, Editor

Barry Seiler, *The Waters of Forgetting*
Raeburn Miller, *The Comma After Love: Selected Poems of Raeburn Miller*
William Greenway, *How the Dead Bury the Dead*
Jon Davis, *Scrimmage of Appetite*
Anita Feng, *Internal Strategies*
Susan Yuzna, *Her Slender Dress*
Raeburn Miller, *The Collected Poems of Raeburn Miller*
Clare Rossini, *Winter Morning with Crow*
Barry Seiler, *Black Leaf*
William Greenway, *Simmer Dim*
Jeanne E. Clark, *Ohio Blue Tips*
Beckian Fritz Goldberg, *Never Be the Horse*
Marlys West, *Notes for a Late-Blooming Martyr*
Dennis Hinrichsen, *Detail from The Garden of Earthly Delights*
Susan Yuzna, *Pale Bird, Spouting Fire*
John Minczeski, *Circle Routes*
Barry Seiler, *Frozen Falls*
Elton Glaser and William Greenway, eds., *I Have My Own Song for It: Modern Poems of Ohio*
Melody Lacina, *Private Hunger*
George Bilgere, *The Good Kiss*
William Greenway, *Ascending Order*
Roger Mitchell, *Delicate Bait*
Lynn Powell, *The Zones of Paradise*
Dennis Hinrichsen, *Cage of Water*
Sharmila Voorakkara, *Fire Wheel*
Kurt Brown, Meg Kearney, Donna Reis, Estha Weiner, eds., *Blues for Bill: A Tribute to William Matthews*
Vern Rutsala, *How We Spent Our Time*
Clare Rossini, *Lingo*
Beckian Fritz Goldberg, *The Book of Accident*
Ashley Capps, *Mistaking the Sea for Green Fields*
Roger Mitchell, *Half/Mask*
Alison Pelegrin, *Big Muddy River of Stars*
Jeff Gundy, *Spoken among the Trees*
Brian Brodeur, *Other Latitudes*